THE CASE FOR
A NEW REFORMATION THEOLOGY

Publisher's Note

THIS BOOK is one of a series of three, written at the request of the publisher: *The Case for Orthodox Theology*, by Edward John Carnell; *The Case for Theology in Liberal Perspective*, by L. Harold DeWolf; and *The Case for a New Reformation Theology*, by William Hordern. They are intended to provide for the lay person, student, teacher, and minister a clear statement of three contemporary theological viewpoints by convinced adherents to these positions.

Each author began with the same description of the purpose of the series and was provided perfect freedom to state his case. No one of the authors, moreover, knew the identity of the other two contributors until after manuscripts were completed; and at no time did any of the three have access to the manuscripts of the others.

THE CASE FOR
A NEW
REFORMATION
THEOLOGY

by

William Hordern

Philadelphia
THE WESTMINSTER PRESS

Hordern, William.
 The case for a new reformation theology.
Philadelphia, Westminster Press [1959]
 173 p. 22 cm.
 Includes bibliography.

 1. Neo-orthodoxy.   1. Title.   11. Title: New reformation theology.
                        Full name: William Edward Hordern.

BT78.H58   230   59–5410‡

Library of Congress

To
Richard Paul

Contents

Preface   9

I. Challenge and Response in Twentieth-Century Theology   11

II. Faith and Reason   31

III. The Nature of Revelation   53

IV. How Can We Know that Revelation Is Revelation?   76

V. God's Immanence and Transcendence   103

VI. Sin   124

VII. Salvation   141

VIII. Conclusion   160

IX. Notes   167

Suggested Readings   172

Index   174

Preface

I was deeply honored by the invitation to participate in this series of books presenting cases for three of the leading theological positions today. But I was also filled with a deeper sense of inadequacy. To me fell the task of speaking for that wide and varied position that has become increasingly popular in recent years. How could any one man present the case for this movement? What could I say that had not been said better by the intellectual giants who have pioneered the position that I am to defend?

My efforts make no claim to originality; every page owes a debt to someone. The footnotes reveal something of this debt, but an unmanageable number of footnotes would have been necessary to tell the full story. If this book has any merit, it lies in the combination that it makes of the insights and wisdom of others. Another defender of the same movement would no doubt make a different combination. It is one of the strengths of what is here called the "new reformation theology" that within it are various strands of emphasis.

I am sure that my collaborators in this series will agree that none of us is primarily concerned with defending a particular school of thought as such. Our task is to understand the Christian truth and insight into life and its meaning. In speaking for a new reformation position, I make no claim that it has any monopoly on such truth. Furthermore, there is no attempt here to construct a complete systematic theology. I have concentrated upon those points where, in my opinion, the new reformation movement has made a particular contribution to theological discussion. Of course there are many other important questions, but space was limited and I thought it wiser to deal more fully with a few key questions than to skim lightly over a more complete number of problems.

I would like to make a special mention of my debt to Edward T. Ramsdell, whose writings made a deep impression upon me. I had the honor of being his colleague for a brief time before his untimely death brought his career to its close. I would have appreciated greatly the further insights that he could have given me upon the ideas here expressed.

I regret that William F. Zuurdeeg's book, *An Analytical Philosophy of Religion* (Abingdon Press, 1958), appeared after my manuscript was completed. His discussion of "convictional language" illuminates many of the things that I try to say upon the topic of faith. He also has many important contributions to make in understanding the significance of analytic philosophy for the study of religion.

I would like to express gratitude to Garrett Biblical Institute for relieving me of my full responsibility during my first quarter there in order that I might finish this work on schedule.

Special gratitude needs to be expressed to my wife, who labored with me over the final draft and the proofreading.

W. H.

I.

Challenge and Response
in Twentieth-Century Theology

Our century has witnessed an amazing revival of interest in theology. This interest is apparent on many levels. The church itself has become increasingly aware of the value of its theological tradition. As a result, the number of first-class minds in the field of theology is as large as at any time in the history of the church. This interest, however, is not limited to ecclesiastical circles. The works of Niebuhr, Tillich, Buber, Maritain, and others are widely read and discussed today in academic circles that ignored theology until recently.

A significant factor in the theological revival is that more and more laymen are becoming interested. A host of books has appeared in recent years to inform the layman about the intellectual basis of his religion. The sale of such books has been impressive. Increasingly, the better colleges and universities are introducing strong departments of religion, and the undergraduates are hungry for theological information, discussion, and criticism. Many a clergyman who has lagged behind the times suddenly finds himself embarrassed by penetrating theological questions from his laymen, particularly the younger people.

This interest in theology becomes even more impressive when we recall to what extent theology was in a state of decline when the century opened. For example, fifty years ago in Biblical studies the primary interest was in "critical" problems, that is, in problems of the authorship, the date, and the authenticity of Biblical passages. Instead of trying to examine the theology of the Bible, scholars were interested in the history of the Hebrew religion, in finding the historical Jesus, and in elaborating the different strands of religion to be found in the Bible (e.g., prophetic versus priestly religion in the Old Testament, and Jesus versus Paul in the New). But today Biblical scholars are pouring forth a flood of books on Biblical theology. Instead of analyzing the Bible into its varying and conflicting parts, scholars have rediscovered its unity.

It is difficult to say precisely why theology has been revived. Partly it is due to the times in which we live. Historical events have forced us back to the ultimate questions of life and its meaning. Partly it is due to the ecumenical movement. At first the ecumenical movement hoped that it could get the churches to co-operate on common action and let the sleeping dogs of theological dispute lie. But it soon became evident that every concern with action is based upon underlying theological presuppositions. The theological issues forced themselves into the open.

But perhaps more important than any of these was the fact that our century inherited a great backlog of unfinished theological business. The eighteenth and nineteenth centuries raised a host of theological problems to challenge the twentieth. In essence the unfinished business forced us to ask how much of the traditional, or orthodox, interpretation of the Christian faith an intelligent man could believe.

The twentieth-century Christian could not ignore the fact that the acids of modernity had been eating away at his faith. Modern science, including the doctrine of evolution, raised serious questions about such Biblical passages as the Creation story, the Fall of man, and the miracles. A scientific spirit had grown up which implied that all events have purely natural causes and can be fully explained without reference to any supernatural forces.

While the scientific world view was taking shape to plague the Christian from the outside, the Bible itself was put under scientific scrutiny within the church. Higher, or historical, criticism was applied to the Bible in the same spirit in which other ancient manuscripts were studied. At many points it became apparent that the Bible was dependent upon religious influences outside the Biblical

tradition. Many traditional beliefs about the Bible were undermined, and Christians were left wondering what authority, if any,
was still left to the Scriptures upon which they had built. The recent
publicity given to the Dead Sea scrolls has dramatized some of the
problems with which theologians have been living for years. Twentieth-century Christians were forced to examine the very foundation of the theological edifice. What is revelation? Can we know
God? And if so, how?

The question of how we can know God raised anew an ancient
theological concern — what is the relationship between faith and
reason? Twentieth-century Christians found themselves in an age
when faith was held in low esteem. If Christianity could not produce rational arguments as sound and critical as those of modern
science, it seemed to many that it must go by default.

And the modern world itself was undergoing a spiritual crisis
that deeply affected the Christian. The nineteenth century had
placed its primary faith in a doctrine of progress. Civilization, it believed, had been moving, was moving, and would continue to move
in a desirable direction. Man, endowed with a scientific knowledge
that was spread by universal education and controlled by democracy, was steadily moving toward the solution of his age-old problems. Man was seen as essentially good, and thus his chief problem
was ignorance. Once man was shown the good, he would do it. But
the twentieth century has not supported man in the manner to
which he had become accustomed. Two world wars, the murder
of six million Jews, the continual threat of atomic annihilation, the
rise of totalitarian regimes, and a host of other ills have filled man
with anxious doubts about his philosophy of life. This anxiety has
been both a challenge and an opportunity for theology.

Theological responses to the threats, challenges, and opportunities
of our time have been rich and varied. We cannot do justice to all
the responses, but three main reactions to the situation can be de-
tected, corresponding to the three volumes published in this series.
Early in the century there grew up a movement, called fundamentalism, that was determined to protect the traditional faith from the
inroads of modern thinking. It was prepared to defy modernity and

let the chips fall where they might. At the same time another theological movement, liberalism, was casting its lot with the modern world, dedicated to the principle that God's truth and scientific truth could not really be in contradiction. Somewhat later in the century, as the catastrophic nature of our times became apparent, another theological movement began to see a deeper profundity in classic Christian thought. Without rejecting the modern world, it tried to re-express the Reformation's insights for the twentieth century. It is this movement with which the present book will deal.[1]

Fundamentalism has had a strange and tragic career. In its sincere attempt to save the traditional faith it emphasized the inerrant nature of the Bible. But in doing this it rejected much of modern science, particularly evolution, and most of the findings of Biblical scholarship. During the twenties it reached the peak of its strength, controlling several Protestant denominations, and successfully conducting heresy trials to keep young men out of the Christian ministry or to eject ordained ministers. Any clergyman who doubted the inerrancy of the Bible, the virgin birth of Christ, substitutionary atonement, or the miracles was in serious trouble.

Fundamentalism defeated itself. Its unrelenting dogmatism, its lack of Christian charity, and its tendency to fight fellow fundamentalists alienated many who might otherwise have been sympathetic to its central aims. Finally, it succeeded in getting laws passed in two states forbidding the teaching of evolution in the public schools. This led to the infamous Scopes Trial in Tennessee, where a young teacher was fined for teaching evolution. Such obscurantism signed the death warrant for fundamentalism, and it steadily lost strength in the major denominations. It lived on in smaller sectarian groups but lacked stability as it divided and subdivided. Having sharpened their teeth in theological battles with the liberals, the fundamentalists began to devour each other. For several years fundamentalism produced no thinkers who won recognition beyond fundamentalist circles, and it was generally ignored in theological debate.

The liberals emerged from the fundamentalist controversy with glowing colors. They were viewed as the martyred defenders of freedom who gladly accepted science and Biblical criticism, and were earnestly engaged in working out a rational defense of the Christian faith built on reason and experience. In many ways liberalism was a mood and a method rather than a system of thought. It was the method of the open-minded search for truth, the willingness to put all ideas, no matter how sacred, to the test of reason. It was opposed to all dogmatism and creedalism. Whereas the fundamentalists found the irreducible minimum of the Christian faith in a set of doctrinal propositions, the liberals found it in the Spirit of Christ. Liberalism, however, did form a basic set of beliefs, influenced by the idealist philosophers.

While liberalism was at the height of its strength, a new foe emerged. The "neo-orthodox" movement made its appearance, charging that liberalism had lost the transcendence of God, the sinfulness of man, the reality of revelation, and Christian eschatology. The pressure of world affairs caused the liberals to do considerable heart-searching at each of these points, and we began to hear of "chastened" liberals, or "neo-liberalism." The new theology, however, continued to make headway against liberalism, setting up its strongholds in many of the seminaries that once had led the liberal forces.

In the present decade the fundamentalist forces made a comeback in theological circles when a group of young scholars began to expound a revised form of fundamentalism. Seminaries like Fuller began to produce scholarly efforts that won attention beyond fundamentalist circles. These new forces were determined not to commit the errors of their fathers. They labored to be scholarly, open-minded, and modern. They found scientists who argue that the Bible and science can be reconciled. Although basically this group stands on the fundamentalist platform, it is a definite revision of the older position. In keeping with contemporary habits in theology we should be calling it "neo-fundamentalism." But the group has a strong distaste for the name "fundamentalist"; so henceforth we shall refer to its spokesmen, as many of them refer to themselves, as conservatives.

The conservative movement has made impressive gains in recent years. Spurred by Billy Graham's success, it has gained a new morale. It publishes the journal *Christianity Today,* which provides a voice for the new scholarship and which has been sent free of charge to most ministers and ministerial students in the country. Slowly other theologians are realizing that this new conservatism is a force with which we must reckon. It is as determined to keep the "fundamentals" of the faith as the earlier fundamentalist movement, but it is more inclined to placate the modern world. It is more optimistic than its predecessors that the "fundamentals" can live with the acids of modernity.

It is against this background that we need to understand the new reformation theology. While the fundamentalist-modernist controversy was at its height, a growing number of Christian thinkers began to find their way to a position that transcended the older controversy. To these men it seemed that fundamentalism had rigidified Christian thinking to the point where it had lost contact with both the modern world and the dynamic riches of traditional thought. On the other hand, it seemed to them that liberalism, in its concern to speak to the modern world, had lost its moorings in traditional Christianity. Although most of the leaders of the new trend came from out of liberalism, they were sharply critical of many aspects of liberalism.

One of the persistent curses in theology is the practice of applying name tags. Almost always this results in sweeping each thinker into the appropriate dustbin and refusing to see the originality and peculiarity of his thought. Thus we call a man fundamentalist and assume that he is a "literalist." We call a man liberal and assume that he has a shallow doctrine of sin. And whoever gets put into the dustbin of "neo-orthodoxy" is guilty, by association, of being an "irrationalist."

The movement that we are defending has, at various times and places, worn such name tags as "Crisis Theology," "Barthianism," "Dialectical Theology," "Neo-supernaturalism," "Theological Realism," "Neo-Protestantism," and a number of others. The most persistent title given to the movement is neo-orthodoxy. This describes the movement, for it has been characterized primarily by a restored interest in the orthodox, or traditional, faith of the church, but it has been orthodoxy rethought and reinterpreted for our times. Having moved in various degrees of liberalism, the heralds of the new system found again the relevance and truth of the Christian tradition. But this did not mean a return to fundamentalism; rather, they were moving " On to Orthodoxy," as one of their proponents put it. But while the term " neo-orthodox " became popular, practically no prominent theologian would allow himself to be called neo-orthodox. The title is used most often as a term of abuse. Undergraduate theological students, looking for a banner to fly, have called themselves neo-orthodox, but few of their leaders have accepted this title.

A major reason for the reluctance to accept the term " neo-orthodox " has been that within the movement there are many sharply distinguished positions. The man who called himself neo-orthodox soon found that everyone assumed that he believed a number of things that, in fact, he rejected. In a former book I suggested that we should also speak of " orthodoxy as a growing tradition " so that we could point up the fact that there is more than one alternative to being liberal or conservative.

The term used in this book, " new reformation theology," has a number of advantages. In the first place, it should be seen, not as a party label, but as descriptive of a mood and trend in theology. It represents an attempt to get back to the faith of the Reformers, but it is not content simply to repeat the Reformers' faith; it seeks to re-express it so that it will be relevant to our century. This term does not lay down any rigid boundary lines. It is broad enough to include many who would prefer to call themselves " neo-liberal " and some who would think of themselves as conservative. No one should be so presumptuous as to suppose that he can speak for the whole of this movement. The present writer claims no more than that he is defending its broad outlines and tendencies.

The attempt to direct our thought to a revitalization of the Reformation is a useful way of getting to the heart of contemporary theology. For one thing, such an approach draws insights from pre-Reformation thinkers, because the Reformers drew heavily upon their predecessors, such as Augustine. Furthermore, we must remember that the Reformation was more than Lutheranism and Calvinism. Often what is called " neo-orthodoxy " has been a neo-Calvinism or a neo-Lutheranism. But the Reformation also included Anglicanism and the sectarian movements. In the minds of many persons the true Reformation was consummated in the Anabaptists, Mennonites, Baptists, Quakers, Congregationalists, and, later, the Methodists. If we are to have a truly new reformation theology, we must include the insights from all wings of the Reformation.

Recent studies of the Reformers have been of great importance for the movement. The Reformation was followed by the period sometimes called " Protestant Scholasticism " or " Protestant Orthodoxy." This was the period in which Protestants became preoccupied with creedal correctness. The Protestant doctrine of salvation through faith came to mean salvation through correct belief. The Protestant emphasis upon the Scriptures became a doctrine about the verbal and infallible inspiration of the words of the Bible. Fundamentalism is a direct inheritor of this scholasticism. To scholasticism it owes its emphasis upon the " fundamentals " of the faith in the form of doctrinal propositions and its view of the inerrant nature of the Bible. Consequently, the new studies of the Reformation have revealed that the Reformers had been lost and perverted in Protestantism. This is why the new concern does not lead back to fundamentalism; fundamentalism is charged with being a Protestant heresy, not the true defender of the faith which it has claimed to be.

The man who goes back to the Reformation finds immediately that he must turn to the Bible, for it was on the Scriptures that the Reformation built. Nothing has been more characteristic of the last forty years in theology than the revived interest in the Bible and its theology. Cause and effect are difficult to separate at this point. Did the new reformation theology create the new Biblical concern or did the rediscovery of the Bible's message and faith create the new reformation theology? One thing is certain: the two interests have overlapped and inspired each other. And here too the findings have been that fundamentalism, claiming to be the Biblical religion, is actually a distortion of the Biblical faith. The liberal used reason and experience to refute the fundamentalist, but the new reformation thinker has used, ironically, the Bible itself to refute the fundamentalist.

The study of the Reformation and of the Bible caused the new reformation thinkers to repudiate fundamentalism or its newer form of conservatism. To this degree they were sympathetic to much in the liberal position. And yet, because fundamentalism was in retreat during the rise of the new reformation position, it was the liberals who received most of the criticism from the newer position. The rebirth of conservatism will help, I believe, to clarify the new reformation position as the mediating position, which it always has been.

The return to the Reformers and the Bible has resulted in certain basic tendencies within the movement. The following themes represent a brief descriptive definition of the movement. They do not exhaust the interests or emphases of its exponents but they do indicate a direction.

In the first place, we find an emphasis upon the fact that we are dependent upon God alone for salvation. The movement has taken with new seriousness the traditional Christian doctrine of sin. In light of this it has affirmed the " otherness," or transcendence, of God. God is not to be equated in any way with man at his best. Consequently, there is no road that leads from man to God. There is not even a two-way street upon which God and man might be able to meet each other. There is only the way from God to man; God in his freedom chooses when and where he will be made known; God always has the initiative in making himself available to man. As a result, man is not saved by his bright thoughts, his good deeds, his church connections, or even by his religious devotions and experiences. This is what it means to take seriously the Reformation doctrine of salvation by grace.

But it is significant to see that the Protestant can face the utter helplessness and sin of man because he believes that the Light has appeared in the darkness and the darkness could not put it out. What man could not do for himself, God has done for him. In Christ, God has invaded our history and made himself known to man. And where God makes himself known it is as the saving God, the God of grace. We have no way of knowing what God will do with man, the sinner, until God himself tells us what he has done. This is what it means to take seriously the Protestant doctrine of *sola Scriptura* (the Scriptures alone).

Man, however, is not a mere bit of flotsam or jetsam that is tossed on the divine waves. Man is created in the image of God, that is, he is created for fellowship with God. When man confesses his sin and dependence upon God, he finds that God grants him all the prizes that he tried to snatch for himself. The reason that could not take man to God is now liberated in the service of God. The man who is subservient to God can never allow himself to be subservient to any human institution, be it the state, the church, or society. No limit can be put upon his freedom of thought and action except the infinite limit of God himself. This is what it means to take seriously the doctrine of the priesthood of all believers.

The history of the new reformation theology is far too complicated to summarize here; we can only indicate a few main trends. Not only are there differing emphases within the general movement, but there are also significant changes within the thinking of individual representatives of the movement. A fascinating story could be written of the changing emphases and conclusions of Karl Barth, Reinhold Niebuhr, and Emil Brunner, just to mention three leaders whose thought has undergone important development.

The movement really began in the nineteenth century in that strange Danish thinker, Sören Kierkegaard. Kierkegaard was a thorn in the flesh of the established state church of his time, but he returned to the Bible and to Luther to find the source of his critique. He attacked the reigning Hegelian philosophy that liberal Christianity used so extensively. He argued that life cannot be forced into a system of rational thought, no man can be summarized as " a paragraph in a system." The basic question that man must ask is the question of how he is to live. An authentic philosophy is a philosophy for life, not for speculation. Kierkegaard scorned the professional thinker who built beautiful palaces of thought and then lived his life in the " dog kennel." Life as it comes to us is not neatly rational; it is paradoxical, and the Christian faith presents us with paradox at its very center — time and eternity united in the God-man. Consequently, faith, or commitment, becomes an important element of philosophy; it is not our task to *find* the truth but to *live* it. We should not worry about what is Christianity but about how do I become Christian?

Kierkegaard broke through the optimistic nineteenth century and dared to expose its dark and seamy interior. He dragged such things as sin, anxiety, despair, and meaninglessness from out of the caves in which his century had hidden them. A few other lonely thinkers joined the protest in his century, particularly Dostoevsky and Nietzsche. But these were all voices crying in the wilderness; the complacent optimism of the times drifted along without paying attention to these prophets. It was not until the twentieth century that men found these strange voices speaking to their condition.

The publication of Karl Barth's *Epistle to the Romans* is usually taken as the twentieth-century beginning of the new reformation movement. But important as that event was, we must not overlook the fact that the trend was already underway before Barth. In Great Britain men like P. T. Forsyth, John Oman, and William Temple were sketching out directions of thought that are certainly in the main stream of the movement. Similarly, in America the real beginning of the movement should be dated from Walter Rauschenbusch's last book, *A Theology for the Social Gospel* (1917). Here we find the beginnings of trends that were to flower a few years later in the thought of Reinhold Niebuhr.

Despite the forerunners, it was Karl Barth who shocked the theological world out of its complacency and made the new theology an official competitor for the Christian mind. Barth began his theological career as an optimistic liberal. But somewhere during the First World War this faith died. In 1918 he published his *Romans,* in which he expressed his new concerns. Much of that book would be repudiated by Barth today, but in it he set the direction of his thought. The Word of God took the central place. God is known only where he speaks and God's Word is spoken in Christ. It is not Jesus, the brilliant teacher and lovable rabbi, to whom we turn but the Word of the living God, spoken through the historical Jesus to contemporary man.

A school of disciples often known as " Crisis Theologians " rapidly gathered about Barth. God, they taught, confronts man and creates a crisis in which man must decide to say yes or no to God. The purpose of the preacher is to force man to face this crisis and to make his decision. Preaching must no longer appeal to man's strength or consist of moral appeals; it must preach to man's weakness, face man with his creatureliness and sin, and point man to his only hope, the work of God in Christ.

The Barthian school, however, soon experienced growing pains, as several of the disciples broke from the master. The most spectacular break was that in which its first mate, Emil Brunner, entered into a sharp debate with Barth over the place of natural theology. Brunner argued that if man has no knowledge of God apart from revelation, man cannot be a sinner until he has heard the gospel. But, said Brunner, God has not left himself without a witness among any people. Barth met this with his famous *Nein!* in which he re-affirmed his faith that we depend wholly upon God for knowledge of God. Brunner, he argued, had lost the doctrine of the Holy Spirit, which tells us that God himself creates his point of contact with man when God desires to speak to him.[2]

Brunner, however, was not lost to the new reformation movement. In this country he became, on the contrary, its most popular European spokesman. Brunner has been a prolific writer and, while he has stood strongly against liberalism, the limited room he gives to natural theology has made him congenial to Americans who were born and raised in liberalism. Brunner has made particular use of Martin Buber's concept of " I and Thou " and has shown how this brings the Biblical revelation alive. In revelation we do not receive supernatural information but we are called to a personal encounter with God.

In the Scandinavian countries the new reformation movement took on a Lutheran form as over against the essential Calvinism of Brunner and Barth. Anders Nygren's work made the terms " *erōs* " and " *agapē* " an indispensable part of the jargon of theological students during the forties. God's love (*agapē*) is distinguished sharply from man's love (*erōs*). *Agapē* is the love that is freely given, that does not wait for an object worthy of love; it is the love that forgives its crucifiers, the love of the Christ who died for us while we were still sinners. *Erōs* always has a calculating element within it; we love that which we find worthy of love. The transcendence of God is pointed up by the fact that his love is not a simple extension of man's love, but is a radically new version of love.

Gustaf Aulén has been prominent in the rediscovery of Luther. In his book *Christus Victor,* Aulén has challenged the claim of conservatives that the Anselmic view of atonement is the truly orthodox view. He argues that the early church and Luther held the classic, or ransom, theory. Aulén's excellent one-volume treatment of systematic theology, *The Faith of the Christian Church,* has become one of the most popular texts in seminaries. It has spread the Lutheran interpretation of the new reformation position far beyond the Lutheran denominations.

Great Britain has contributed many notable scholars to the movement. In typical British fashion, these thinkers have refused to follow either American or Continental extremes but have tried to work out their own peculiarly mediating position. Forsyth, Oman, and Temple have been followed by John and Donald Baillie. John Baillie has summarized the newer views of revelation for us in a masterful fashion, and Donald Baillie's *God Was in Christ* stands as one of the most influential works on Christology in the new reformation movement. J. S. Whale has contributed both popular interpretations and historical studies to the trend. D. R. Davies and many others could be mentioned.

In America, Reinhold Niebuhr has been one of the main leaders. Today Niebuhr tells us that he has never been a theologian, that he is simply a professor of Christian ethics who has also dealt with apologetics. I hope that Niebuhr will forgive us for disagreeing with him. Although Niebuhr has been too preoccupied with the practical concerns of social life to develop a careful theological system, he has brought the deepest theological questions into the open and has shed considerable light upon them. From his early epic book,

Moral Man and Immoral Society, Niebuhr has written his theology always from a social base. The questions that concern him have been those raised by politics and economics. But Niebuhr has found that such questions force him into the theological realm, and so, almost in spite of himself, Niebuhr has been a theological prophet. Because of his concerns, Niebuhr's greatest contributions have been in the realm of the doctrine of man. He has forced us to see that in the affairs of society the traditional Christian doctrine of sin is a more realistic analysis of man than any of the modern alternatives put forward in either liberal theology or liberal political thought.

H. Richard Niebuhr, also starting from an ethical base, has made his own unique contribution to the movement. Other Americans who have contributed to the movement are John Mackay, Edwin Lewis, and Wilhelm Pauck. If one were to include the younger men making names for themselves within the movement, the list could go on for another page. There are three other names that must be mentioned although none of the three has allied himself specifically with the new movement: John C. Bennett, Walter Horton, and Nels Ferré have made important contributions to a reawakening appreciation of the Reformation. These men are usually called liberals or neo-liberals, but, as we have said, an advantage of speaking about a new reformation theology is that it enables us to describe a wider trend than is implied by the party name, neo-orthodoxy.

Two brilliant names are conspicuously absent from this roll call of the leaders of the movement. Although the new reformation theology has learned much from Rudolf Bultmann and Paul Tillich, it cannot claim either man. Bultmann, the New Testament scholar, has developed a new theological movement, generally referred to as demythologization. If the gospel is to speak to modern man, says Bultmann, it has to be demythologized. The result is a gospel interpreted primarily in terms of Heidegger's existentialist philosophy. Early in his career Bultmann was an enthusiastic follower of Barth, but today he is seen by Barth as originating a new liberalism. Whereas earlier liberalism built on idealist philosophy, Bultmann builds on Heidegger.

Paul Tillich for many years was considered a neo-orthodox theologian in America although in Europe he was considered a liberal. He himself has argued that he stands on the border line between liberalism and neo-orthodoxy. But in recent years it has become evident that he is drifting farther from the neo-orthodox border line. It is interesting and informative to watch the growing gap between the thinking of Reinhold Niebuhr and Tillich.[3] Tillich's reliance on ontological analysis, neo-Platonism, and idealistic philosophy make it difficult to include him within our new reformation framework, despite the contribution that he has made to clarifying the " Protestant principle." Although liberalism and conservatism are the chief competitors to the new reformation position considered in this series, it should be noted that Bultmann and Tillich quite possibly will be the most formidable competitors to the position in the years to come.

On the American scene a major development in the history of the new reformation movement is now unfolding. Karl Barth's voluminous work, *Church Dogmatics,* is being translated into English. Most Americans have held a stereotype of Barth, formed on the basis of his *Romans* and his critics' version of him. But today, as we see the mature Barth, we find ourselves in the embarrassing position that all our stock arguments against him are irrelevant. The target has moved. It will be interesting to see if a new wave of Barthianism will follow this publication.

We have sketched the general theological background out of which the new reformation theology has emerged. Before turning to our defense for this position, it would be well to examine some nontheological influences.

Theologians have failed, generally speaking, to take with sufficient seriousness the implications of the revolution that has occurred in philosophy. Liberal theology, in its attempt to make Christianity relevant to the modern world, allied itself with idealism, which was the dominant movement in philosophy. This seemed logical, for although there was a tension between idealism and Christianity, there were many points of contact. The idealist was a colleague in the battle against materialism and naturalism. The Absolute of idealism seemed to have common properties with the God of Christianity, so that arguments for the Absolute could be transposed into arguments for God. There were times, of course, when the Absolute took the place of the Christian God, but on the whole the liberals worked faithfully to make idealism the handmaiden who would serve Christ, even as Aquinas used Aristotle. More recently liberals have often leaned on philosophers like Bergson or Whitehead. Paul Tillich has used the metaphysical systems of neo-Platonism, German idealism, and existentialism.

In so using philosophy, liberalism took a calculated risk. The liberals were aware that there was a tension between their Biblical faith and the God they could produce from out of their philosophy. There was always the danger that they would end up with more of idealism or of Whitehead than of Christ. But the advantage was that they could speak to the modern age; they were showing the intellectual respectability of Christianity. They did not ask modern man, with his suspicion of faith, to start with faith; they were prepared to reason with him and to take him, by reason, to the point where faith would be a reasonable next step.

Karl Barth followed Kierkegaard in criticizing this alliance of theology and philosophy. Barth insisted that this alliance could do nothing but distort the Biblical faith. You cannot serve two masters; if you start with Whitehead or Royce, you will not end with Christ. There is no correlation between the Absolute or the Principle of Concretion and the living God, who reveals himself where he wills to reveal himself. And so in theology today there rages the debate between so-called philosophical theologians who would combine theology and philosophy, and " kerygmatic," or Biblical, theologians, who would preach the Christian gospel without aid from philosophy.

The irony of this debate in theology lies in the fact that it is, with the exception of a few British theologians, conducted in almost complete disregard for the contemporary scene in philosophy. The philosophy about which the theologians debate has nothing to do with philosophy as it is being taught in an increasing number of the better philosophical departments in our colleges and universities. If one searches the leading philosophical periodicals for references to the philosophers upon whom our philosophical theologians lean, he probably will search in vain.

One of the major developments that has occurred in philosophy has been the death of idealism. Although, as philosopher Morton White comments, some American universities "have established reservations for dying philosophical races like idealism," [4] the movement has lost its vitality and ability to inspire the younger philosophers. The death of idealism might not be too serious, but with it has died metaphysical philosophy as such. In Europe an anti-metaphysical form of existentialism holds the stage while in Anglo-Saxon countries the dominant mood is that of language analysis. In a series of books on philosophy through the ages, the book on the twentieth century is called, appropriately, *The Age of Analysis*.

Many theologians seem to be acquainted only with the early expression of the new philosophy — that of the Vienna Circle — logical positivism. But most of the critiques made of logical positivism in theological works are outdated. Few philosophers stand today with the early Carnap, Schlick, or Ayer. The primary task of philosophy is now seen to be the analysis of language, and in this process most metaphysical speculations are found to be nonsensical and meaningless.

Most theologians are aware that the traditional philosophical proofs of God have been in a shambles since the days of Kant and Hume. They do not seem to be as aware, however, that the various alternatives to the traditional proofs have fared even worse at the hands of the analytic philosophers. As John Hick says, theologians have been slow to grasp the significance of the fact that, philosophically speaking, we must build our theologies without proofs.[5] Contemporary philosophy forces us to confess that we have no scales "in which to measure, for example, the evidential weight of apparent universal mechanism against that of the impact of Christ upon his disciples." [6]

I am not claiming that the last word has been spoken on the matter of metaphysics by the analytic philosophers, although I agree with them. But we do have to face this paradoxical situation. The philosophical and rationalist theologian today is farther from the contemporary philosopher and seems to the philosopher to commit more logical blunders than the Biblical theologian. The calculated risk of the theologian who built on the metaphysics of idealism or Whitehead may have seemed justified in the days when such an alliance enabled the theologian to talk with the contemporary philosopher. But it hardly seems justified in a day when such metaphysics are as much of a scandal to the modern mind as the Biblical faith itself.

It is not strange that the liberal theologians have been reluctant to accept the new trends in philosophy. To accept the new philosophy would require the liberal to give up his claim that he built his theology on a rational foundation. But it is strange that the new reformation theologians have not been more aware of the philosophical change. The new philosophy is not so radically different from all past movements as it likes to think. William of Occam in the Middle Ages is an interesting forerunner. To the man who returns to the Reformation it ought to be significant that Luther proclaimed himself an Occamite. If Luther could work with Occam's philosophy, the new reformation theologian should find himself at home with the analytic philosopher.

One reason that new reformation theologians may have been slow to recognize the worth of the new philosophy is that in its earliest form, logical positivism, it seemed to make revelation as meaningless as metaphysics. And so J. V. L. Casserley argued that the attack on language is equally urgent for theology and metaphysics.[7] But this logical positivism was based, as logical positivists were forced to admit, upon a metaphysical system itself. Today the former logical positivist, A. J. Ayer, concedes that language may have other meanings than those of science, but the man who claims this must show how he would verify his language.[8] In other words, the analytic philosopher of today is no longer dogmatically legislating as to what can be meaningful. He does show the absurdity of trying to go from science or common sense to metaphysics, but he leaves open the possibility of the metaphysician finding another stepladder.

This is still a challenge to theology, but it does mean that a theology like Karl Barth's can live with analytic philosophy. Barth has never claimed any scientific or philosophical verification for his faith; he never committed that logical blunder. The Christian faith, insists Barth, has its own means of verification. In other words, Barth has been seeking to verify the Christian faith along the precise lines that the analytic philosopher admits to be possible, at least in theory. Barth is in further conformity with the analytic philosophy in that where the philosopher sees his task as that of analyzing language in general, Barth sees his task as theologian to be that of analyzing the language of the church.[9] Analytic philosophy is a challenge to theology today, but, ironically, it would seem that the kerygmatic theologian, Barth, is better equipped to meet the challenge than most of the philosophical theologians.

Many new reformation theologians have ignored analytic philosophy because of their preoccupation with existentialist philosophy. From the existentialists the movement has reaped many benefits. The existentialist analysis of modern man's anxiety, estrangement, and desperate longing for a meaning to life makes an interesting background for the Christian gospel. But I agree with Barth that existentialism can be as dangerous to a new reformation faith as was idealism. From Kierkegaard we have learned much, but it is from Kierkegaard the Christian thinker, not Kierkegaard the existentialist philosopher. The following pages will reveal that I owe a real debt to existentialists, but I must confess that I have turned with relief from their turgid attempts at digging up their souls by the roots to see if they are growing to the brittle clarity of the analytic tradition.

In its history Christianity has used and laid aside many philosophies. Some of these have been helpful, some have been dangerous, all have been held in some degree of tension with the faith. The most serious danger is to suppose that Christianity stands or falls with any particular philosophy. Today I agree with John Hick that there is an opportunity to see the theological right illuminated by the philosophical left.[10]

The analytic philosophy, despite its skepticism, is less dangerous to the faith than former philosophies that theology has used. It does not stand on a metaphysical basis; it does not offer a rival interpretation of life. These philosophers are not, as Basil Mitchell points out, occupying a rival pulpit and preaching a rival faith.[11] On the other hand, the theologian is uniquely concerned with the problem of language, and it would be strange if he did not find welcome aid from the philosopher who has made it his task to analyze language and its meaning. As Prof. W. F. Zuurdeeg suggests, analytic philosophy and new reformation theology can have a mutually stimulating co-existence.

This summary of the present scene in philosophy leads to our first problem — the relationship between reason and faith in knowing God. The contemporary philosopher throws serious doubt upon the claim that we can build a purely rational foundation for a metaphysics or a world view. If contemporary philosophy is correct, then the so-called philosophical, or rational, theologian is operating on the basis of faith as much as is the kerygmatic, or Biblical, theologian. This will be the first thesis of our apologetic.

II.

Faith and Reason

TWENTIETH-CENTURY theology has been preoccupied with the problems of theological method expressed particularly in the form of a debate about reason and faith. Liberal theologians have seen ominous dangers of irrationalism in neo-orthodoxy while the neo-orthodox have argued that the rationalism of the liberals destroys the Christian faith. Barth and Brunner, long theological allies, came to the parting of the ways over the question of what part, if any, a rational system, or natural theology, could play in Christian thought. This is no new debate in Christian history, but the modern age has given it a new urgency.

Liberalism generally has insisted that reason is vital and necessary to theology. Without reason, it is argued, we cannot judge between various claims to revelation; we are at the mercy of the first fanatic who comes along claiming to have a revelation. It is superstitious and immoral to hold a faith that does not have a rational basis. Every advance made by man has been made by the application of reason to his problems. If theology does not use reason, it can only lead to a new dark age. And so neo-orthodoxy is charged with having brought about a " religious revolt against reason." [1]

Over against the liberals are those, often called " fideist," who have insisted that faith must be primary. Man is in no position to judge God; he is judged by God. If liberals have a rational criterion to judge revelation, they do not need revelation; the criterion is higher than revelation. A vital relationship to God demands a decision, a commitment, but reason does not end with a commitment; it ends with a conclusion. A man may rationally prove something to be true and good and still make no commitment to it. When sinful man makes reason his primary source of knowing God, he idolatrously creates God in his own image, he creates the God that he wants to worship. Reason forms its systems, sets its standards, and then demands that God fit the standards that it has erected. Instead of accepting God on God's terms, it insists upon God meeting our terms.

One reads the conflicting claims and is impressed with the convincing case that each side can make. And then it becomes clear that the two sides seldom come to grips with each other. What one side condemns as reason or faith is not what the other side extols. Therefore, if there is to be more light than heat, we must analyze carefully the meaning of the terms in order to isolate the real issues.

Reason, like many aspects of life that we deal with daily, is difficult to define precisely. Reason is the activity whereby man tries to organize, interpret, and understand his environment. It includes the use of logic, argumentation, inference, deduction, induction and so on. By reason we analyze and synthesize the elements of our experience to understand and comprehend the world.

There are many paths by which reason may arrive at understanding. There are, for example, scientific experimentation, pragmatism, the rule of logical coherence, and so on. But central to all types of reason is the drawing of conclusions by some method of logic from some set of given propositions and/or facts. It is thus the essence of reason that it implies universalism. If an argument is truly rational, it will persuade all qualified persons. Furthermore, reason in the nature of the case aims to be objective; the emotions and desires of the reasoning man must not change the conclusions to which rational thought leads.

So defined, I think that it is evident that any person who thinks or who tries to communicate his thoughts must use reason. Furthermore, I know of no responsible theologian who would deny that reason is an indispensable tool of theology. Often those theologians who, like Kierkegaard, use paradox are called " irrational." But, as Martin Heinecken shows, paradox in Kierkegaard's thought depends upon reason. Paradox is the point where reason humbly confesses that God is beyond our comprehension. " It is really quite amazing why anyone should seriously object to the admission of such a possibility and should condemn it as a cult of irrationalism. . . . All that is meant is that a man should admit he is confronted with something the intellect cannot handle, and how else could he be persuaded more convincingly than by means of the absolute paradox?"[2] We may or may not accept Kierkegaard's point, but we cannot call it irrational. On the contrary, Kierkegaard has as much of a stake in reason as any liberal. If irrationalism is accepted, there is no significance in a paradox. But Kierkegaard is convinced that there is great significance in the paradoxical; so he has to take the claims of reason seriously. In short, Kierkegaard's use of paradox is a highly rational procedure; it is reason's way of pointing to the mystery of God.

I find little evidence that there is a religious revolt against reason. Barth is often charged with being a foe of reason, but Barth has never suggested that reason is not to be used as a tool in theology. Actually, one of the strongest defenses of reason in modern theology is found in Barth, who deplores the de-emphasis upon the intellect in religion.[3] And thus he argues that whatever it is, Rudolf Otto's " numinous " is not the Word of God because it is the " irrational."[4]

The question is not, Will theology use reason? but, Is a natural theology possible? Natural theology seeks a knowledge of God found without any appeal to revelation or faith. It would be a knowledge of God arrived at through appeals to evidence and logic that are available to all rational men. It is natural theology in this sense that Barth denies. But, as we shall try to show, it does not follow that because a man denies natural theology he is irrational.

Faith is more difficult to define than reason. We live in a culture that uses the term " faith " in ways that distort the Christian meaning. We commonly say that we have knowledge where we have complete evidence for something. Where we have good but not complete or irrefutable evidence, we say that we believe. And where we have little or no evidence for something, we say that we " have faith " in it. Faith thus becomes associated with the lowest grade of evidence. It is close to superstition, " woman's intuition," emotionalism, and wishful thinking.

Wherever there is this popular view of faith, a theology that builds upon faith will naturally be held in suspicion. L. H. DeWolf has defined faith as " a commitment of the will to an object not indisputably proved worthy of such commitment," or support of a judgment or belief " not indisputably proved to be true." [5] With this definition of faith, it is natural that he finds fideists to be revolting against reason, for he sees a lack of evidence as a defining principle of faith. But it is difficult to find any theologian who is building on faith in this sense.

There are actually at least three meanings of religious faith, and we should have three words to distinguish them. We might call them *credentia, fiducia, and fides*.[6] By *credentia* I mean the acceptance of propositions, information, conclusions, directions, etc., without demanding normal evidence or proof. *Credentia* is the " faith " that accepts an authoritarian rule. Protestantism has little place for *credentia*. Luther protested against the authoritarianism of the Roman church, but it was, I believe, a betrayal of the Reformation when Protestants insisted upon *credentia* in the writings of the Bible. To accept any statement because " the Bible says so " is *credentia*.

Protestantism, from Luther on, has asserted that faith is not the acceptance of unproved dogmas, but that it is *fiducia*, trust. To have faith in God is to trust God, to take him at his word. But when we trust someone, we commit ourselves. To have *fiducia* is to make a decision. This means that faith is never simply belief. Of course, faith normally includes some belief, but it cannot be identified with belief. When Paul is speaking about faith, it is quite evident that he is not preaching salvation through belief. For example, he can say, " I am crucified with Christ: nevertheless I live; yet not I, but Christ liveth in me: and the life which I now live in the flesh I live by the faith of the Son of God, who loved me, and gave himself for me " (Gal. 2:20). Paul is not speaking about belief intellectually held; he is pointing to a radical reorientation of the whole direction of life. The commitment of faith is one so radical that Paul can speak of his old self as crucified. No matter what a man may believe or know, he does not have faith until he has taken the " leap of faith " and committed his life to what is believed or known. As John Wesley put it, faith " is not barely a speculative, rational thing, a cold, lifeless assent, a train of ideas in the head; but also a disposition of the heart." [7]

But there is a further element to faith as it is used by fideist theologians. Faith also contains a cognitive element, it is not only *fiducia,* it is also *fides.* For example, Gustaf Aulén says, " Whatever else faith may say about itself, it does not say that it is some sort of subordinate knowledge, a kind of uncertain opinion about God and his work." [8] On the contrary, as Luther put it, God and faith belong together, for faith implies a relationship to God. We cannot speak about faith without being conscious of man's relationship to God. What is signified by faith is therefore a " personal fellowship between God and man." [9] When the new reformation writers speak about the primacy of faith, they do not mean the primacy of uncertain beliefs; they mean the primacy of a particular cognitive claim. Faith is a way of knowing.

Karl Barth's name usually leads all the rest when liberals are denouncing the men who have made theology irrational. But this interpretation comes from reading " faith " in Barth's writings as *credentia.* An analysis of what Barth means will reveal that this is not what he is saying. For Barth the Word of God, spoken to man through the Bible, is not something to be accepted because the Bible has authority or because the church says so. On the contrary, it is accepted only because it comes with its own cognitive claim upon us. " It comes to us as a datum." [10] That is, it is analogous to our statements about the physical world. As sensory data are cognitive raw material, so is faith. Faith is a cognitive relationship to a reality beyond ourselves. This is why, although the Reformers emphasized faith as trust or decision, they also affirmed that faith is a gift. In faith man makes his decision, but he does it in the light of something given to him; he is confronted; he is gripped by that to which he commits himself.

It is significant that Barth insists that this knowledge which comes through faith must immediately be examined by reason. " It would not be a serious awareness of this reality were it not immediately to turn to understanding also." [11] Barth further clarifies his concept of reason and faith when he says, " If we would or could merely be aware without wanting to understand, merely let ourselves be told without also telling ourselves what had been told, merely have faith without knowledge, it certainly would not be God's revelation with which we had to do." [12] In short, Barth does not call us to swallow some set of doctrines or conclusions. He witnesses to the fact that God is made known to man through faith. And this faith immediately moves man to seek understanding. Reason does not produce the faith, but reason is necessary to comprehend what has been disclosed. This is no more irrational than is the scientist who begins with his sensory perceptions, accepts them as objective, and then seeks to understand them.

There is a reason for the misunderstanding of those called fideist. From Luther to Barth we find such men often making sharp attacks upon " reason." Reason is referred to as a " whore," and faith is extolled because it takes reason by the throat and strangles the beast. Such language often leaves the impression that these men are calling us to the deathbed of all rational thought. If our aim is simply to get rid of them by branding them as irrational, we can find plenty of quotes for our ammunition. But if we really desire to come to grips with what they are saying, we must see their words in context. None of them has argued for a theology without reason.

What those called fideist have been denying is that man has, within himself and his material world, the means whereby he can build a ladder from earth to heaven and gain some knowledge of God. They claim that our knowledge of God must come from God himself. This is why faith must have its cognitive element. Knowledge of God has to be given to us, for we never possess this within ourselves. We do not find God as a thing within the physical world, because God is not a thing. God is the Lord and he is the Creator; he is not, therefore, to be found as a part of this world, nor is he to be inferred from it. In other words, if God is not found at the beginning of our process of reasoning, he cannot be dragged in at the conclusion as an inference from something less than himself.

The natural theologian, whether Thomist or Protestant, usually believes that the finite world can give us some clue to God. There is an analogy between the cause and the effect. By examining the world (i.e., the effect) we can reason analogously to the cause (God). This method, often referred to as the *analogia entis* (analogy of being), runs into difficulties. Logic tells us that we can prove nothing by analogy.[13] To be persuasive an analogy must be based on considerable knowledge of both sides of the analogy. We cannot say that because every event in the universe has a cause, so the universe must have a cause, for we do not know whether the universe is an "effect." If we had several universes and each of them had a cause, we could argue by analogy that this universe also has a cause. But when we have only one universe, we have no way of knowing whether or not it needs a cause. Similarly, we cannot say that all designs have designers, the universe is a design, therefore it has a designer; for, as Hume showed in his *Dialogues Concerning Natural Religion,* we can explain the universe as well if we assume that it is a vegetable or an animal as we can by assuming that it is a design. In short, if we have no knowledge of God when we begin, analogy cannot give us any knowledge about him.

Therefore, Barth has suggested that we need to use the analogy of faith. That is, only after God reveals himself can man speak analogously about God because only then does he know what kind of analogy will fit. This is an attack upon reason only in the sense that it recognizes the limits of reason. Reason can deal only with that which is given to it, and therefore it cannot speak about God until he has given himself to it. Unless reason is illuminated from God's side, it cannot get to God.

The natural theologian is disposed to boast that he lays a rational foundation under his religion; he is not like the fideist who superstitiously begins with faith. But this claim must be taken with a grain of salt. If the analytic philosopher is right, it is the natural theologian who commits the greatest crime against reason. Any rational arguments that he uses to establish belief in God are found to be not only illogical but also nonsensical.[14] This may not be a final disproof of natural theology, but it is strange, to say the least, that the philosophical theologian's arguments are declared unphilosophical by capable philosophers. This is not analogous to two scientists disagreeing about the effects to be expected from atomic radiation. This is as if one of the scientists in the dispute were denying the ability of science to deal with the question. In this situation it seems dubious that the philosophical theologian can claim to be more rational than the fideist.

We do not escape this dilemma by doing as Tillich does. He grants the philosopher that we cannot prove God's existence, but he tries to restore a natural theology through an " ontological analysis." But renaming metaphysics and calling it ontology does not satisfy the philosopher. He still finds Tillich guilty of logical confusion.

What do we make of this situation? We can try to outargue the analytic philosopher, although personally I find the natural theologian's replies unconvincing. Or we can, as most natural theologians are doing, ignore analytic philosophy, but that is the very obscurantism that the natural theologian condemns in others. Or we may say that the analytic philosopher works with presuppositions that we do not accept. But what does this mean? It means that the faith from which one begins to reason predetermines the outcome. The natural theologian must then admit that he begins with a faith, and only if you accept his faith, can you come to his conclusions. He is not so different from the fideist as he has pretended to be.

Even if one does not accept the arguments of the analytic philosopher, his very existence proves an important point. The natural theologian's reason is incapable of persuading all rational men. In fact, he fails to make them see that there is even a sensible argument to be discussed. What can we conclude but that something more than reason is involved in this? As I shall try to show, the problem is not that we all can reason to some point and then some may go on in faith and some may not. The situation is that every act of reason is an act performed in the light of a faith. The natural theologian, no less than Barth or the analytic philosopher, begins with faith.

The position that I wish to defend is that reason and faith cannot be separated any more than the modern physicist can separate space and time. Of course, for the purpose of analysis, we can distinguish between them, but in a living situation they are never to be found apart. Every act of faith is an act that only a rational creature could make, and hence involves reason. But every act of reasoning involves an act of faith. Reason and faith are not exclusive principles between which we must choose; they are aspects of life that go hand in hand.

This position, often called Augustinian, is expressed by the slogans, " Faith seeking understanding " or " I have faith in order that I may know." These slogans show the intimate relation of reason and faith. They recognize the presence of faith in every act of knowing, and they see that it is of the nature of faith to seek understanding.

To say " I have faith in order that I may know " is to argue that every act of reasoning is preceded or accompanied by an act of faith. In our context this is to say that reason presupposes a cognitive experience which leads to an act of trustful decision. Since the days of Thomas Aquinas it has been widely held that we can start thinking with reason alone. The religious rationalist has argued, therefore, that we ought to go as far as reason can take us in gaining knowledge about God. After we have done this, it is then rational to go on with faith and accept what has not been proved by reason, although even here one should aim to keep his faith in harmony with the findings of reason. Thus Aquinas believed that reason alone can prove that God exists but it is only by faith, accepting revelation, that we can know that God exists as a Trinity. Liberal theology generally has taken the attitude that reason comes first and that we are justified in having faith only after reason reaches its limits. It is our thesis that this is a mistaken conception.

If faith comes after reason, then it inevitably has an element of *credentia,* and is distinguished from the findings of reason by the fact that it lacks the degree of verification that reason gives. But it is our thesis that faith as cognition, trust, and commitment comes not after but before and with reason. It is the prerational framework within which reason operates. It is not a conclusion lacking verification; it is the frame of reference which decides what the criteria are that will verify. It is the presupposition of all verification. So considered, it is not true, as often claimed, that the Christian operates on faith and the atheist does not. Before discussing the nature of Christian faith, therefore, I shall try to indicate how a faith element operates in all reasoning.

A mathematician, Frank De Sua, writes:

> " Suppose we loosely define a *religion* as any discipline whose foundations rest on an element of faith, irrespective of any element of reason which may be present. Quantum mechanics, for example, would be a religion under this definition. But mathematics would hold the unique position of being the only branch of theology possessing a rigorous demonstration of the fact that it should be so classified." [15]

And it is a philosopher, Victor Kraft, who says:

> " If we regard a proposition about a repeatedly tested state of affairs as indubitable, this is because we presuppose that things have not changed in the meantime, that there is uniformity in the world, i.e., that there are laws in the world. But this presupposition itself cannot be known to be true with certainty. . . . That the unexpected will not happen, we cannot know for certain. It is an article of faith, so firm that we even risk our life on it, but it is not a proposition that could be proved." [16]

In other words, even the most rigorously rational enterprises — mathematics, science, and philosophy — begin their reasoning in the light of a faith. All of their proofs rest finally in a frame of reference that cannot be proved.

It might be objected that while no doubt science and mathematics make presuppositions, they hardly need " faith " in the way in which we have defined it. But I think that we can argue that this is at least analogous to the operation of Christian faith, viewed from its human side. The scientist begins with a basic trustful commitment of the self. The scientist is committed to the premise that it is possible and that it is good to treat the world rationally. If someone objects to the whole scientific enterprise by saying, " Where ignorance is bliss, 'tis folly to be wise," there is no scientific answer. The objector has denied the relevance of anything that science could say. And in an age of hydrogen bombs and the displacement of men and honored occupations by mechanisms, in the hustle, rush, and anxiety of modern life with its increase of mental disturbance over that of primitive societies, it can hardly be claimed to be self-evident that science is valuable. The scientist must work with a faith-commitment to the value of science whether the faith be explicit or implicit. But the commitment does not end here. A philosopher, Richard Von Mises reminds us that every act of induction, so central to the reasoning of the scientist, involves an act of personal decision.[17]

Central to Augustine's concept of reason was his conviction that the will is prior to knowledge. " Before I can know, I must will to know." The terminology is somewhat dated, but, as John Hutchison has suggested, what philosophers traditionally have called the " will " might be called " the active or functioning unity of the human self." [18] That is, the self does makes decisions, and whatever this decision-making power is, that is what Augustine meant by the " will." Today we are inclined to believe that the whole of a human person is involved in his decisions — his reason, emotions, and all other aspects of his being. Reasoning is always the act of a self, and it is, therefore, dependent upon the decision of the thinker.

The function of the " will " is evident to anyone who has been in a classroom. The correlation between achievement and native intelligence is far from complete, because motivation plays an important part in any process of learning or thinking. If a man has no will to know something, he will not bother to think about it.

The modern world has made a great deal of " objectivity," the position of detachment from which the learner must approach knowledge. The objective man is one who has no prior commitments, who does not allow his wishes to affect his conclusions; he simply " lets the facts speak for themselves." This is seen as the ideal of the scientist, and it is argued that it should be the ideal for all scholarship. Because of this, one often hears college students arguing that an atheist would be a more objective professor of religion than a Christian because the Christian already has committed himself to a religion while the atheist is " unbiased." But if Augustine is right, and experience seems to prove that he is, this is a naïve view.

In any subject matter a man must be committed in the sense that he is sufficiently attracted by the subject matter to commit himself to studying it; he wills to know. Thus we hear the scientist praised in one breath as the great example of objectivity, and in the next breath he is hailed for his noble dedication (i.e., commitment) to science. If an atheist were really uncommitted in religion, he could not have enough interest in the subject to know it. To say that such a man should teach religion is like saying that a witch doctor should teach physics because he has made no commitment to any of the theories of modern physicists. On the other hand, if the atheist is committed to religion, so that he has willed to know it, then he cannot be judged a priori to have any less " bias " than the Christian. One man is committed to atheism, the other man to Christianity. Either or neither may be a good teacher of religion.

In the light of what has been said, it is well to take a further look at the popular cry of " let the facts speak for themselves." It is obvious that the one thing facts cannot do is speak for themselves. Facts have to be interpreted and understood, for knowledge is never a simple snapshot of reality; it is always an interpretation. But an interpretation implies that one has a frame of reference, a basic perspective, within which he interprets the facts. I once heard a scientist say that science has countless facts to which it pays no attention because it has no frame of reference in which they can be interpreted. It is interesting to note that he said this during a discussion of the many facts claimed by various forms of psychic research. Because such facts do not fit into the frame of reference with which the scientist operates, he ignores them.

G. K. Chesterton, in his vivid manner of speaking, insists that it is quite wrong to say that the madman has lost his reason; he has lost everything but his reason. This recalls the classic story of the psychiatrist's patient who thought that he was dead. The psychiatrist told him, " You know that dead men do not bleed, don't you? " The man agreed, so the psychiatrist triumphantly pricked the man's finger, and as the man watched the blood come, he shook his head in bewilderment and said: " What do you know? Dead men do bleed! " The man's reason was perfect; it was his frame of reference that was defective. Hume demonstrated that our thinking about the world always operates within the framework of certain basic perspectives about the nature of causality, the external world, the unity of the self, and so on. Reason does not establish these; they are the basic framework within which reason works; if a man denies them, there are no arguments by which they can be established. In other words, when the facts speak for themselves, what they say depends upon the frame of reference within which they "speak" as well as what the facts actually are.[19]

Another annoying aspect of facts is that, as E. T. Ramsdell has made so clear, they do not come before us with marks to denote their relative significance.[20] One set of facts points to conclusion A and another set to conclusion B, but which is the more significant? The facts cannot decide that; we must make a decision and we make it in the light of our frame of reference. This judgment of relative significance plays a crucial part in all thinking. We tend to perceive and to remember only those things which we deem significant (a fact that causes much trouble between men and their wives). And consequently, the varying interpretations of the same set of facts is most often the result of differing estimates of their relative significance.

This is why the cult of objectivity in education can be dangerous. When a teacher prides himself upon objectivity, he hides both from himself and others the frame of reference within which he approaches the facts and by which he selects the facts that seem to be significant. As a result, he gives his findings an aura of finality that they do not deserve. The danger is that the student will accept his teacher's prejudices because they seem to be the necessary result of rational thought. This is why I believe that the most truly objective teaching can occur only where the professor honestly confesses the frame of reference to which he is committed. Having done this, he should try to present as sympathetically as possible all opposing positions. But because his students know his frame of reference, they can guard against the inevitable bias that will appear.

In short, instead of being impossible where there is a faith-commitment, objectivity is possible only where a faith-commitment is made to objectivity. Objectivity is never a matter of reason alone; it requires a moral decision on the part of the self. It is the good man rather than the brilliant thinker who can achieve it in the highest degree. But the man who claims that his thinking is purely objective, that he has no frame of reference, or who claims that he has the only possible frame of reference — this man is simply demanding that his frame of reference and evaluation of relative significance must be adopted by all men who are to think. This is why the most prejudiced thinking is quite frequently dressed up in the robes of objectivity. This is also why the self-styled "rationalist" often holds his religious beliefs in the most dogmatic fashion.

If so much depends upon a man's will and his frame of reference, what do they depend upon in their turn? Obviously they are grounded upon the whole experience of a man's life. Ramsdell says "reasoning never occurs in the abstract. It is always the activity of an individual mind. It can never be separated from the crucial experience of a particular living person. . . . What we evaluate as meaningful is inextricably bound up with our total life as persons." [21] We all have had the experience of disliking some subject although we had heard many arguments why it was important for us. Then one day we were fortunate enough to have a teacher who made the subject live for us. Suddenly our wills were motivated; we longed to know. It was not that the facts of the subject matter were changed. We still needed to sit down as a little child before the facts, but the perspective from which we viewed them was changed and their significance for us was completely new. We looked at the old subject matter in a new light because we had been confronted by something that we had missed before. It was not the result of a logical argument; it was, rather, that the facts "gripped" us in a new manner. This experience, common to most men, provides an analogy to what I have called the *fides* element in religious faith. The religious man witnesses that certain facts, overlooked as insignificant by the irreligious, have gripped him; he has been confronted by a new significance in them.

In other words, reason is never productive by itself, for experience in some sense must precede reason. We cannot reason about the Christian faith, for example, until the Christian faith has been given to us to reason about. This may sound so obvious that it appears to be trivial, but precisely because it is so obvious it is often overlooked. Reason does not start from scratch and work out its systems by pure logic. Every line of reasoning presupposes the total experience of the person who is reasoning; it works in direct correlation with what life has presented to us and with what has impressed us as being significant.

What we have been saying about the reasoning process is true, I believe, for all types of thought. But it is obviously more important for thinking in some fields than in others. In some areas the frame of reference is of minimum importance, since there may be no serious alternatives. This is most likely to be the case in mathematics and the natural sciences, where man is not so crucially involved in the subject matter. But certainly as we move into the social sciences and the humanities, a man's frame of reference becomes more and more crucial, and his abstract arguments will have less and less persuasive power. It is an obvious fact that a man's environment, profession, and personal experience play a large role in his political decisions. When, however, we come to the religious questions of life, we are dealing with a man's ultimate frame of reference, his ultimate criteria of what makes life significant and meaningful. At this level the role played by the frame of reference is most crucial.

In forming a religion, or one's ultimate relationship to life, no facts can be eliminated, for all are potentially relevant. But obviously all cannot be dealt with equally; a decision must be made as to their relative significance. The philosophy or religion by which a man lives can never be the simple result of letting facts speak for themselves; it is, on the contrary, the principle by which he chooses and selects the facts that are considered significant.

The attempts to prove God's existence illustrate our point. The various " proofs " have been argued from both sides *ad infinitum* but they seldom persuade anyone. It is not difficult to see why this is the case. We must look to the whole of reality to decide our question. But within the totality of reality we find many facts. The theist accepts the teleological argument because he finds that the facts showing order in the universe are the most significant. But the skeptic points to the facts of disorder and they seem more significant to him. No appeal to the facts can solve this dilemma, for both sets of facts are equally real. The question is, Which are the more significant? The theist may turn to religious experience to prove God because he finds such experience the most important and significant fact in his life. But the skeptic rejects the argument because the appeal is to " subjective " experience and the unbeliever's frame of reference is such that he believes that only facts that are open to public observation are significant. Again no facts can decide, for what is at stake is not the facts. The unbeliever will concede that the believer has probably had some deep personal experience. What is at stake is the frame of reference that decides which facts are significant. If the unbeliever were to have the believer's experience, he might change his opinion, but no argument alone can change it.

In short, the very idea of proving God presupposes that there is some common neutral arena into which believer and unbeliever alike can come to settle the question rationally. But each man comes wearing his particular set of spectacles that colors everything that he sees. This is why increasingly those philosophers of religion who still consider the proofs of God as important see their importance not as arguments, but as analyzing what we mean when we speak about God. They cannot establish faith in God; they explicate what it involves.

J. C. Smart says that if someone asks, " Do electrons exist? " the question is meaningless by itself. In order to answer it you need a lot of experience with physics, experiments, cathode-ray tubes, and so on. When we get this experience, we find that the concept of electrons is a useful and indispensable item in physical theory. At this stage the question of whether electrons exist no longer rises. Before this, it is a meaningless question. From this he concludes:

> " Similarly, I suggest the question ' Does God exist? ' has no clear meaning for the unconverted. But for the converted the question no longer arises. . . . Within religion the question ' Does God exist? ' does not arise any more than the question ' Do electrons

exist? ' arises within physics. Outside religion the question 'Does God exist? ' has as little meaning as the question 'Do electrons exist? ' as asked by the scientifically ignorant." [22]

In other words, a man can raise the question of God's existence only from out of the context of his whole life and experience. The man who has been confronted by God in the context of the Christian church and its revelation cannot pretend that he does not bring this experience with him to any discussion of God, for it is precisely this experience which has formed his view of what is ultimately significant in life. On the other hand, the unbeliever cannot pretend that he comes to the debate apart from the context of his life in which he has made his ultimate faith commitment to an other than God.

There is a further implication in Smart's point. Because of the different experience from which men come, the " God " discussed in a philosophical debate is not necessarily the God of faith. In many a philosophical discussion of God, the Christian feels like Mary before the tomb: " They have taken away my Lord, and I know not where they have laid him." What does the First Cause, the Absolute, the abstract God of speculation, have to do with him " who so loved the world, that he gave his only begotten Son "? This is why Pascal called upon the God of Abraham, Isaac, and Jacob, the God who revealed himself in the life of a historical community, not the God of the philosophers. Paul Tillich has argued that the God of the philosophers is the same as the God of the prophets, but Will Herberg counters very effectively by simply asking, " Which philosophers? " [23] It may be that philosophers who have the Judaeo-Christian God in their experience are speaking about Abraham's God, but to say that all philosophers are doing so is to ignore the realities.

An analogy may help to make our point. I recall a picture that appears to be a black-and-white landscape, but you are told that, when rightly seen, it is a portrait of Christ. So you sit looking at the picture and feeling sillier and sillier as someone says, " Look, here are his eyes and his mouth," but still you cannot see it. Then suddenly something comes into focus and the portrait of Jesus stands out clearly, and you wonder at your stupidity in not seeing it before. You see the same lines as before, but the whole perspective and the significance of the lines have changed. The *Gestalt* is completely different.

This illustration is symbolic of what Christianity itself is like. The first disciples knew Jesus the man; they met in him a new and moving experience. Then suddenly their eyes were opened and they saw, with Peter, " Thou art the Christ, the Son of the living God." The facts were not materially different for Peter than they were for Caiaphas, but Peter's perspective enabled him to see what Caiaphas' perspective forced him to miss. This was the point that the Reformers made. We do not become Christians because our reason has been persuaded by a brilliant argument. Rather, we are " converted "; in the experience of life a light breaks and we see what we did not see; we are no longer blind. And just as I was not aware of doing anything when the portrait of Christ came into focus, so Luther and Calvin affirmed that faith is a gift. That is, something happens to us in the light of which faith is born.

Man finds himself in a universe that bombards him with experience. At an early date he begins to find significance in these experiences; they are saying something to him. He begins the mysterious process of coming to know. No one does, or can, pay attention to everything that comes to him as experiential raw material; he begins to interpret and select his experience in terms of relative significance. We can see this by comparing the sensitivities of a primitive man and a civilized man. Their potentialities are so developed that in the face of the same experiential raw material they will see, hear, smell, and think about different things.

In the process of coming to know his world, man begins to develop his frame of reference, his judgments of relative significance. Certain things grip him; to him they seem ultimately significant, and so he trusts them, he commits his life to them, he has a faith. Reason does not establish this faith; on the contrary, this is what gives a light to his reason. This faith may be implicit or it may be explicitly developed. But life has to be lived and this means that the faith must enable one to live meaningfully, and so it has to seek understanding.

When a faith seeks understanding, it may fail. It may be unable to incorporate a man's experience meaningfully within its framework. When this occurs it becomes increasingly difficult to live by the faith, and two things may happen. A man may close his eyes to more and more of the facts of his life and live by just those facts which his faith can comprehend. Or he may undergo the costly and difficult decision to change his faith. He is converted.

Many theological rationalists argue that we must test all beliefs in terms of whether they fit together coherently with each other and with experience. That system is most likely to be true which is the most comprehensively coherent. Of course, in one sense the test of coherence is a tautology; to think means to think coherently; there is no other way of thinking. But as an ultimate test of truth, coherence runs into a practical difficulty. When a man faces a fact that does not fit coherently into his preconceptions, he can do one of two things: he can deny the significance of the new fact and ignore it as the scientist ignores the findings of psychic research, or he can change his preconceptions so that the new fact will be contained coherently. But which he does cannot be decided by the claims of coherence, for both alternatives result in a coherent system. Which he does will depend upon his will, his decision, and his *fides* experience.

The point, of course, is that a man's faith succeeds or fails, not in the forming of a coherent system of thought, but in the living of life. Our position is existential in that it sees that man's faith is something that must be lived and that comes out of life. Religion is never worked out like a syllogism of logic; it is hammered out in the experiences of life; it is a matter of life and death. It is the perspective from which we view life, in the light of which we make our decisions, and by which we live. It is when a faith fails at this level that it is abandoned. Several former communists wrote a book with the suggestive title *The God That Failed*. The "God" in this case was the communist faith. Here we get case studies in what happens when a man changes his ultimate philosophy of life; he finds that in the task of living his god has failed him. Instead of illuminating his life, his ultimate faith becomes itself a major problem.

There are many ways in which a " god " may fail a man, but generally speaking it occurs when experience causes a man to see a new significance in certain facts. We sometimes sneer at the way in which people turn to religion when death or disaster strikes. We called it " foxhole " religion a few years ago. Of course it may be shallow, but it is not necessarily so. Many persons can live with their faith until they experience tragedy for themselves. At that point their faith is revealed to be inadequate. We have always known that tragedy is a part of life, but now it is *my* tragedy, and the perspective by which one lives is put to a crucial test. And there is no simple logic here — the tragedy that brings one man to God will drive another man away.

But it is not only tragedy, for the joys of life can also bring a man to see that his faith cannot find understanding. Sometimes it is falling in love, having a child, meeting a new appreciation of beauty and joy, which changes our faith. In short, there are many experiences of life that can disrupt a man's frame of reference, but it is doubtful that any ultimate frame of reference can be undermined except by life itself.

It is not unusual, however, for a man's " god " to fail without the man's recognizing that this has happened. He goes on living his life and hiding his eyes from realities that face him. It is here that a negative apologetic can be useful. Many twentieth-century men were living by the faith that society was continually progressing. This was their basic frame of reference in the light of which they saw the significance of all facts. The twentieth century's history made this faith more and more difficult to square with the facts. But many continued living by the faith until Reinhold Niebuhr's apologetic drove home to them the incongruity between their faith and their life. Of course, even here, the rational argument has its limits; the man may still argue that the twentieth century's ills are but the birth pangs of the new era of utopia. But the facts of life along with the critique may lead a man to adopt a new perspective.

This explains why we "witness" to our faith. We do not have iron-clad proof and we cannot assure a man of the truth of a religious faith, but we witness to it. We try to show him how life looks and is lived from the perspective of our faith, and then we invite him to take his "leap of faith" and to stand where we stand. We have to have enough confidence in our faith to believe that if a man does that, he too will come to see its truth.

One of the main reasons that we cannot prove the truth of the Christian faith to the man outside is, of course, that our criteria of judgment have to be changed. Accepting Christianity brings a radical change in a man's set of values. Things that were formerly thought to be valuable and significant are now seen as worthless. (Phil. 3:7-8.) But until this change has occurred, it is difficult to persuade the man that Christianity is superior to his present frame of reference. To the man whose first allegiance is to economic success, the acid question is, Will it make me more wealthy? To the man who worships pleasure, the acid test is, Will I have more fun? The man who worships science will want to know what scientific problems a Christian faith can help to solve. And so each man from his particular perspective scans the Christian faith and asks if it can meet his present wishes, desires, and evaluations of significance. This creates a serious temptation to the Christian, and today there are many who are ready to give a glib "yes" to such questions. Become a Christian, we are told, you will be happy, healthy, wealthy, popular; you will have peace of mind and serene security. In short, man is promised that Christianity will give him everything that he has wanted most as an unbeliever. But it is impossible to verify one frame of reference by the criteria of an alien frame of reference, and the attempt to do so can only lead to disillusionment.

In summary, we have argued that faith implies both *fides,* a cognitive relationship, and *fiducia,* a trustful decision to commit oneself. Faith, so defined, naturally seeks understanding, and so it reasons. The Christian faith is not something that goes beyond what reason attains; it is a perspective within which reason works. All reasoning operates on the basis of a cognitive relationship to reality out of which is formed a perspective, a frame of reference, by which the relative significance of facts is judged. On the basis of this perspective a man makes his trustful commitment; he wills to know. As Ramsdell has put it:

> "It is not a matter of rationality but of the perspective of rationality. It is never, at bottom, a matter of the opposition between faith and reason but rather between the faiths which define the divergent perspectives of reason. The natural man is no less certainly a man of faith than the spiritual, but his faith is in the ultimacy of something other than the Word of God. The spiritual man is no less certainly a man of reason than the natural, but his reason, like that of every man, functions within the perspective of his faith." [24]

We shall try to see in the following chapters what is the nature of the particular faith-perspective of Christianity and how it finds understanding.

III.

The Nature of Revelation

Closely related to the questions of faith and reason is the question of revelation. How is God made known to man? Twentieth-century theology has been deeply concerned with this question, and it may well be that its greatest contributions to posterity will be made in this area. The question was posed by the intellectual developments of the last two centuries. Christianity, a religion based upon the faith that God was revealed through history, found its Scriptures subjected to radical historical criticism. In an age geared to scientific and rational thought, the Christian faith would be an insult to intelligence if it asked that certain truths be accepted without undergoing the normal means of verification.

Revelation was a basic issue in the fundamentalist-modernist controversy. Fundamentalism denied the relevance of a historical criticism of the Scriptures; it insisted that the Bible contained an inerrant message from God. Liberalism insisted that honesty forced us to admit that the Bible was a fallible book, with internal contradictions and statements that had been proved wrong by science and historical research. Fundamentalism preserved the Christian faith in revelation but did it in such a manner that it led to open conflict with science and scholarship. Liberalism accepted science and historical criticism, but it was often embarrassed to explain in what sense the Bible was a necessary source of knowledge about God.

Basically the liberals tried to find a subjective refuge from the threats to the faith. Following Schleiermacher's emphasis upon religious experience and Ritschl's emphasis upon moral experience or value judgments, liberals found the vindication of their faith within their own experience. Instead of faith resting upon miraculously verified events of the past, it rested upon what happens within a man's heart here and now. Such a refuge from the threats of historical criticism is tempting, and we find both Bultmann and Tillich still exploring this possibility.

It is doubtful, however, if the Christian faith can take this way out. This method always runs the danger of wishful thinking — what objective check is there to man's inner feelings? Furthermore, the Christian faith claims that God became man. If he did, we cannot escape from the fact that God put himself fully into our human midst. As no legion of angels swept out of the skies to save Jesus from the cross, neither can a legion of mystical angels save the record of his life from being subjected to historical criticism. If we take seriously the faith that God revealed himself through a historical person, we cannot long comfort ourselves with the idea that our faith can live no matter what history says about this person.[1]

Where liberalism tended toward subjectivity, fundamentalism strived after pure objectivity. God's revelation, it affirmed, is objectively present in the words of the Bible, attested by divine miracle. But whereas liberalism left a question about objective criteria, fundamentalism left a problem of the subjective. What has this historical record of long ago to do with me here and now? Does not the living God have a Word to speak to the twentieth century or has he spoken and fallen into silence?

In this situation a new reformation theology must strive to preserve the Reformation's faith in the objectivity of revelation given through the Scriptures. And it must do justice to the subjective facts of revelation; the objective revelation must be witnessed to by the Holy Spirit, as the Reformers affirmed. To meet the present century this Reformation faith must be expressed in the light of the new situation that we face because of the development of historical criticism and modern thought in general.

Revelation means an unveiling, the making known of that which was formerly unknown. As a result, it is not uncommon to hear any new knowledge called revelation. Nature, we are told, reveals its secrets to the scientist. In fact, liberalism with its immanent view of God often argued that there is no basic difference between the revelation of God and the revelation of knowledge about nature. But the term " revelation," as I would define it, can be used of scientific knowledge only in a metaphorical sense because it implies activity on the part of a revealer. We do not normally think of nature taking the initiative to make itself known. Nature just is, and man may or may not discover its secrets; it depends upon man. If God simply waits until man, on his own initiative, discovers whatever clues to his nature God may have dropped when he created the universe, then we can use the term "revelation" in theology only inexactly.

The term "revelation" implies a view that God is, in some sense at least, personal. John Baillie says: " For the revelation of which the Bible speaks is always such as has place within a personal relationship. It is not the revelation of an object to a subject, but a revelation from subject to subject, a revelation of mind to mind." [2] It is the prerogative of a person to reveal himself. We take the initiative in revealing more of ourselves to some people than to others. Thus we speak of "revealing circumstances," incidents in which a person through his behavior or words reveals himself and his nature with particular clarity. Of course finite human persons often reveal themselves inadvertently; they let slip a word, or thoughtlessly perform an act that drops the veil from their character. But if God is truly the Lord, we cannot suppose that he reveals himself except where he wills it. If there is revelation of God, it can be only because God took the initiative to make himself known to man.

Revelation is a personal act of disclosing that which is otherwise unknown. But the great question is, What does God reveal? For many centuries it was taken for granted that what God reveals is information that can be put into rational propositions like any other knowledge. In fact, it has not been unusual for persons holding this view to argue that some of the information revealed by God is such that man could have discovered it for himself, but God, in his goodness, revealed it so that the wise would have no advantage over the ignorant.

Where revelation is believed to be items of information in the form of propositions, the proper response to it is humble belief. Consequently, wherever this view has been held, faith usually has come to mean belief (*credentia*). If God reveals information, we almost have to accept the view that the revelation is infallible. As the fundamentalist says, if you deny any statements in the Bible, you are calling God a liar. In fundamentalism and conservatism this view is carried to its conclusion by insisting that although the Bible is not a book of science, nonetheless any statements that it makes in this area are preserved from error.[3]

A cogent argument for informational revelation is made by the Roman Catholic theologian, Victor White. He admits that faith is more than assent to propositions, but he insists that it does not follow that we can dispose of verbal teachings. The revelation of Christ must be communicated to me if I am to live it, and it must be communicated accurately. It is not enough for my salvation that Christ lived and died, but I must know this fact and I must know who Christ was and is. Furthermore, I cannot do the will of God unless I know his will, and I cannot receive his grace unless I know where he has chosen to give it to me. Thus White says:

"Words, spoken or written, are still indispensable to *convey* the Word, the Christ-fact, to us. He himself, while still living and working amongst us, *speaks;* speaks human words to convey divine truths about himself and his Kingdom: the truths about our own selves and the way whereby we are to receive his salvation."[4]

The disciples, continues White, were called to tell others what they had received; they were to take Jesus' place when he was gone and to speak with his authority. But the disciples had no authority to teach whatever they wanted; they were to teach the gospel that they had received. Therefore, they had to teach with infallibility. They were not given verbal dictation, but they were so assisted by God that they were incapable of error in their apostolic function. Thus the Bible was infallibly inspired, but the need for infallibility did not end there, as was shown by the rise of heretics who misinterpreted the Bible. Consequently, the church has inherited the apostle's authority in order that it may interpret the Scriptures accurately.

This is a strong rational argument. If we grant the premise that God has imparted to man certain information that is necessary for salvation, the rest follows with stunning logic. Obviously, such important information cannot be at the mercy of the vicissitudes that haunt normal pieces of information. Protestant fundamentalism or conservatism is made to seem incomplete. Even if the Bible is inerrant, how can we know which of the conflicting interpretations of the Bible is correct? Does each reader of the Bible become a pope who can interpret it infallibly? The Roman Catholic seems to have an unanswerable point when he insists that if an infallible revelation is necessary at all, there must be a continuing infallibility.

It is no wonder that such an argument has persuaded many through the centuries. The strongest answer to it is to challenge its basic premise — that what God reveals is information, and this we shall do later. But here we might note that for all of its strength, the argument runs into serious problems.

First of all, it tends to lead to idolatry of the Bible and/or the church. A man's relationship to the church's teaching or his stand on the Bible becomes the acid test. Instead of asking whether he has faith in God, he is asked if he accepts the teachings of the church or of the Bible. The church and the Bible are beyond all possible criticism; they are absolutes in and of themselves. Instead of pointing to the absoluteness of God, they now share his absoluteness.

Secondly, although the view always claims to be the preserver of the unity and the catholicity of the church, it inevitably leads to division. From an early time the church lacked true catholicity. The more authoritatively the church taught, the less true unity it had. This is evident in the rise of Montanists, Donatists, Albigensians, Waldensians, and the rest. For a time the grim hand of political authoritarianism could give a false vision of unity, but beneath lay the rebellion that broke loose as soon as there was freedom to do so. Similarly, fundamentalism has divided and subdivided. And there is good reason why this is so. If you believe that you possess

the infallible information necessary for salvation, it is difficult to
have fellowship with any man who denies the least jot or tittle of
what you proclaim.

The doctrine of infallible propositional revelation has become
more and more difficult to hold in the face of modern knowledge.
This is the view that has been involved in the science-religion debates of recent centuries. It has presented an unenlightened critique
of the findings of Biblical scholarship. It is significant that conservatism has retreated to the point where it admits that no manuscript of the Bible that we now possess is inerrant. Only the original
manuscripts, now lost, were without error. Since that time copyists
have made mistakes, so that no existing manuscript is perfect. But,
it is affirmed, God has kept this process under control, so that there
has been no error in any doctrine necessary for man's salvation.[5]
This concession, however, obviously leads to the subjective influences that the conservative has tried to avoid. How do we decide
what is necessary for salvation and hence free from error?

One of the gravest problems of the concept of inerrant propositional revelation is in the question of what it means. Man always
has a tendency to take a magical view of words as if they had some
kind of power and being in their own right. But words and propositions have only one purpose — to communicate from one person to
another by pointing to a reality beyond themselves. Thus I cannot
sit on " chair "; it is simply the symbol that I use in communica-
tion with others to point to the object upon which I can sit. A
proposition is a tool; it has a task to perform, and to perform its
task it must be spoken and it must be received.

When a proposition is spoken, however, it is affected by the
hearer. No matter how carefully we choose our words, they run the
continual risk of being interpreted differently from what we intended. If we think of propositions independently of their environment and not engaged in doing what propositions are meant to do,
then we might refer to them as inerrant. That is, they are absolutely correct words to refer to the objects desired by the speaker,
even though no one has understood them. But if we think of
propositions acting as propositions are meant to act, what does it

mean to call them inerrant? The fact that they may have issued from the speaker " infallibly " is irrelevant unless they come into the understanding of the hearer meaning precisely what the speaker meant by them. In short, to call a proposition inerrant, and to mean anything serious about reality in the statement, we must mean that it is not only spoken to express infallibly what the speaker wants to say, we must also say that it is impossible to hear it otherwise than as the speaker intended it to be heard.

But no defender of inerrant propositional revelation has pretended that all hearers of the propositions understood them perfectly. The Bible is understood differently by different people. And Roman Catholicism does not solve this dilemma by its claim that the church must interpret the Bible infallibly. It only shifts the problem from the Bible to the church. It is impossible to claim that everyone who has heard the church's infallible declaration of doctrine has found the same meaning in it. Not only do those outside the church fail to see the meaning, but even within Catholicism there are wide differences of opinion as to the meaning of the declared doctrines and, worse still, debates as to what has been declared doctrine and is hence infallible.

In short, I find serious confusion in the very concept of an inerrantly revealed proposition. If anyone, for any reason, fails to understand what God desired to have understood in the proposition, then it can be called inerrant only in a strained and unreal sense. It has not performed inerrantly what it was meant to perform. Earlier we mentioned that fundamentalism tried to give an objective defense against Biblical criticism, but now we can see why this is not enough. An objective revelation is not inerrant until it is inerrantly received. The subjective receiver of revelation is an indispensable link in the chain. As Kierkegaard put it, there is no truth until there is truth to me. If there is to be inerrant revelation of propositions, the hearer would have to be as inerrant as the speaker. If man is not infallible, and seldom have Roman Catholics or fundamentalists claimed infallibility for the hearer, then it may be emotionally comforting to claim that God spoke without error, but it is meaningless to us men who are fallible hearers, for we can never know infallibly that we understand correctly the infallible revelation.

The practical problems involved are well illustrated by the long debate between science and Genesis. For example, Genesis says that God created the world in six days. (Gen. 1:1 to 2:3.) This seems to be a simple enough statement; it means that in a period of one hundred and forty-four hours God completed creation. And so Christians interpreted it for centuries. When science first began to show that the events of Genesis must have taken longer than this interpretation implied, fundamentalists rejected the idea. But scientific evidence became more and more convincing. Then fundamentalists decided that a " day " in Genesis did not mean twenty-four hours but a period of indefinite time. Similarly, the Genesis story seems to teach that God created each separate species and again most Christians so understood it. But when the evolutionary theory became too much to resist, the conservatives found that God created " kinds," not species, and the evolution may have occurred within these kinds.[6]

Finally, Carl Henry, summarizing the agonizing of the conservatives over Genesis and science, suggests that although science must not be permitted to fix the content of revelation, " it is welcomed as a negative check against false exegesis." [7] In other words, Genesis is an inerrant picture of creation, but the Christian cannot know what it means until the " assured results " of science come in. This means that the doctrine of Scriptural inerrancy has become a purely emotive reaction to the Bible; it can give no practical knowledge since we must await science to see if our exegesis is correct. Worse still, it would seem that the words of the Bible can be stretched to mean anything that, in view of science, they " should " mean.

Such dilemmas might have been avoided if Protestants had remembered the emphasis of the Reformers that the Holy Spirit must illuminate the heart of the reader if he is to hear the Word of God in the Scriptures. Thus Calvin says that, " if we were inclined to argue the point," there are certain arguments that we could bring forward to indicate that God is speaking in Scripture. But Calvin hastens to say that " yet it is acting a preposterous part, to endeavor to produce sound faith in the Scripture by disputations." Men, he tells us, cannot have Christian faith if they are persuaded by arguments, even arguments from Scripture. "The testimony of the Spirit is superior to all reason. For as God alone is a sufficient witness of himself in his own word, so also the word will never gain credit in the hearts of men, till it be confirmed by the internal testimony of the Spirit." [8] Furthermore, when Calvin begins his chapter on "Rational Proofs to Establish the Belief of the Scripture," he opens it with the warning that all such arguments are vain without something more than such arguments. And he concludes it by again affirming that, without the Holy Spirit's witness, belief in the Scriptures will be in vain.[9] This is equally clear in the thought of Luther who always affirmed that in Scripture, it is only God himself, who can tell us that this is God speaking.

If the Word of God is heard only where and when the Holy Spirit illuminates the receiver of revelation, then it is not crucial whether or not the propositions involved are inerrant. In fact, we may insist that the man who reads them without the guidance of the Holy Spirit cannot hear what God intended to say through them and so for him they cannot be inerrant. But, just as God became man and revealed himself through the limited human person of Jesus, so the Holy Spirit can speak to us through these human and finite words.

We have seen difficulties in the view of an infallible revelation of propositions. These difficulties are not likely to persuade the believer in such revelation to give up his belief, but they are sufficient to make the concept impossible for many persons in our age. Many find that intellectual integrity will not allow them to accept propositions that strain their credulity just because some authority tells them that they must accept them. But the strongest argument against this view is the showing of an alternative.

Faced with the dilemmas and the problems that we have seen, and rediscovering the views of the Reformers, modern theologians have presented a new understanding of the nature of revelation. This view has been most adequately summarized by saying that what God reveals is not propositions or information — what God reveals is God. In revelation we do not receive a doctrine or some esoteric piece of information that man's wisdom could not have discovered. In revelation we are brought into a living relationship with the person of God. God's Word never consists of black marks on the pages of a book called the Bible; God's Word is the living Word which he speaks through the Bible and to which man must respond by saying yes or no.

This view has been developed through many creative thinkers. Sören Kierkegaard, Martin Buber, Karl Barth, Emil Brunner, Richard Niebuhr, William Temple, and others have made their particular contributions. Although the view is in many ways a twentieth-century development, it can, in all fairness, be claimed that it is true to the Biblical view and to the view of the Reformers.

Central to this viewpoint is the recognition that there is a basic difference between the way in which we know things and the way in which we know persons. No doubt the distinction between " I-it " and " I-thou " relationships has been overemphasized by some thinkers, but the distinction is necessary. To know things I need I.Q. and training; to know persons I need to be a self; I need moral character. I know things by observing them, experimenting with them, and I seek to know them in order that I may be able to manipulate them. But to know a person I must enter into fellowship and communion with him; there has to be give and take. Of course my relationship with another person may be an I-it relation; I may think of him and treat him as a thing. When that happens, although I may gain extensive information about him, I do not know him as a person. We can know *about* things and, in impersonal relations with persons, we know *about* persons. But we can only *know* persons.

The importance of this for theology has been pointed up by Buber, who has shown that there is no analogy between knowing the Biblical God and knowing things, but there is a real analogy between knowing God and knowing persons. One of the services that analytic philosophy renders to theology is to help us see that so long as we try to speak about God as we speak about things, we end up in speaking nonsense.[10] John Wisdom, in a lecture, pointed out that the question, Is there a God? is in no sense like the question, Are there cookies in the jar in the cupboard? The Biblical God never appears as a thing or an object to be studied. Theology has little to learn from philosophy's discussion of how we know things. But there is much to be learned from the problem of how we know "other minds."

In our relationship with the God of revelation, we are not called into an I-it relation with the First Cause; rather, we are called into a personal relation with the Father of Jesus Christ. Jesus did not say, "Blessed are the brilliant: for they shall logically prove God's existence"; he said, "Blessed are the pure in heart: for they shall see God" (Matt. 5:8). In personal relations the purity of one's heart is a vital factor in knowing. That is, love, moral integrity, imagination, empathy, are needed to know a person as they are not needed to know a thing. When God's revelation comes to us, it does not come as propositions to subdue the mind; it comes as a challenge to the "heart," it appeals to the whole man. The faith to which it calls us is not the submissive believing of propositions but the commitment of the self in trust to the God who is encountered. The view of propositional revelation distorts this by directing our attention to an I-it relation with a book, a church, or a creed.

Theology and creeds are man-made devices to point to the fact of God's revelation of himself. As Barth puts it, they are witnesses to revelation. They are useful to the degree that they can point beyond themselves to God, but we should never commit the idolatry of mistaking them for revelation. God reveals himself in order that, through fellowship with him, man's life might be renewed, redeemed, saved. But propositions cannot do this; they can only point to it.

Even in our relationships with other persons, we find that propositions are grossly inadequate to express the reality that we know. This is why we turn to poetry, to symbolic actions, and to anecdotes to express what we know about the uniqueness of the other person. A police description of a young girl might be scientifically accurate, but her mother and her lover would agree that it failed to do justice to her reality. How much less can we expect propositions to do justice to the reality of God's person! Most Christians would agree that John's proposition, "God is love" (I John 4:8), is an excellent description of God as revealed in Scripture. But we cannot consider it infallible. To many a hearer it will convey the wrong impression, because the word "love" today has many connotations that cannot be applied to God. To know what love means in this context we have to point to the acts of God in revelation — to his choosing of the Jews, to Jesus' relationships with little children, to the woman taken in adultery, and to the Pharisees. Finally, and above all, we must see its meaning in Jesus' death and in the Bible's interpretation of the meaning of that death.

There is another way of approaching the problem. In collecting new items of knowledge, the collector of knowledge does not normally change. He increases his volume of knowledge, but he remains essentially what he was before. Knowledge may broaden a man, but his center can remain stationary. But the whole point of knowing God is that it changes the man, the center of his life is shifted. It may or may not add new information to a man's store of knowledge. Referring back to our discussion of the faith-reason problem, revelation occurs when a man's perspective or frame of reference is changed. "I was blind, but now I see," he cries; the face of Christ appears in place of the landscape.

Many persons saw Jesus when he lived; they saw his acts and heard his words, but they found in him no revelation of God. Pilate's experience was broadened through his contact with Jesus; he had a new set of anecdotes to tell at the drinking parties in Rome, but Pilate heard no revelation, no Word of God. At first the disciples were in the same situation as Pilate. They were deeply impressed by Jesus as a man, so impressed that they sacrificed much to follow him. But one day, faced by the challenge of Jesus' question about who men said he was, Peter confessed, "Thou art the Christ, the Son of the living God" (Matt. 16:16). And Jesus tells him that flesh and blood have not revealed this to him, but God himself. This incident might well form the text for the position we are defending. The believer in propositional revelation is trying to find revelation in the equivalent of "flesh and blood," that is, in the words of Scripture or the church. But revelation is revelation only when it is made known by God himself, that is, through the Holy Spirit.

Peter is the rock upon which the church is founded, not because he was the first pope, but because every Christian must come to revelation as Peter came. Like Peter, we must first see the man, Jesus. Here is the objective side of revelation; this is the givenness of God's action. But God is hidden as well as revealed in Jesus; many had seen Jesus without hearing the Word of God. As God awakened the response of faith in Peter's heart, so he must awaken it in each Christian's heart.

We do not see Jesus in the flesh, as did Peter; we must read about him in the Bible. This is why the Bible is the indispensable medium of God's revelation; it alone records the events through which God was revealed. In the Bible we read the witness of the Biblical writers that through this Jesus of Nazareth God's revelation came to them. In the Old Testament we find the preparation for this revelation, and in the New Testament we see it received and accepted. But we may read the Bible from cover to cover and never hear the Word of God. On the other hand, at any moment God may use a word of the Bible to speak his Word to our hearts, and in that moment we can confess, with Peter, "Thou art the Christ." This, I believe, is what Luther had in mind when he called the Bible the crib that holds Christ. The Bible is the earthen vessel through which at any moment God may speak to man. (II Cor. 4:7.)

Barth and others have seen a parallel between the doctrine of Christ and the doctrine of revelation. The church has been forced to combat two heresies about Christ. One denies his divinity, and the other denies his humanity. Either claim would destroy the Christian faith. Both these heresies arose in the early church, and both have been persistent ever since. If the church has had difficulty in persuading unbelievers that Christ is divine, it has had almost equal difficulty in persuading believers that he is truly human. Of course, ever since the early creeds were established, most Christians have paid lip service to the humanity of Jesus, but in thought and speech there has often been an implicit denial of true humanity. It is significant that the full implications of the church's belief about Christ did not appear until after heresies had arisen, that is, until explicit positions were put forward that were recognized as destructive of the faith.

I suggested earlier that the twentieth century's chief contribution to theology might be in its analysis of revelation. In fact, I believe that it may be doing for the Bible and revelation what the first six centuries did for Christology. And it can do this, not because the men of our century are wiser than men in earlier centuries, but because, as the early centuries had to face the twin Christological heresies, so our century has had to face opposing heresies about the Bible.

The rise of Biblical criticism brought to the fore two sharply opposed positions. On the one hand, there were many liberals who could no longer find revelation in any meaningful sense in the Bible. It was an impressive book of human wisdom but not essentially different from other human writings. It represented a particularly fruitful search by man for knowledge of God and moral values. Immediately this position was opposed by fundamentalism and conservatism. Whereas some of the liberals saw the Bible as a purely human book, just as some had seen Jesus as simply a human being, the conservatives followed a path similar to that of the Docetists and denied the true humanity of the Bible. It is true that conservatives have been most careful to insist that they do see a human element in the Bible. They do not want to argue that the Biblical writers were only dictaphones transcribing God's words. But, as many pay lip service to the humanity of Jesus and then deny it in practice, so the conservative position often denies in effect the true humanity of the Biblical writings. God so overwhelmed the humanity of the writers that the normal tendency to err was erased.[11] And what conservatives do for the Bible the Catholic position does for the church.

The new reformation position arose in this century in answer to these two viewpoints. Against all who would deny divine revelation in the Bible, the twentieth century has rediscovered the Word of

God speaking through the Bible. In the Bible we find recorded the unique events, the mighty acts, through which God revealed himself to man, and we meet the witness of the writers to whom God spoke through these events. The Bible is not man's noble search for God; it is God's gracious search for man. But, thanks to the higher criticism of the Bible, we can no longer ignore the completely human element that entered into its writing. Whatever may be the ultimate fate of current views in Biblical criticism, we cannot lose sight of the fact that the Bible is a human book, arising in human situations, and written by human men with all the frailties of finiteness.

Barth has a way sometimes of overstating his case, but these words of his are a healthy antidote to the claims of an infallible propositional revelation:

> "Every time we turn the Word of God into an infallible Biblical word of man or the Biblical word of man into an infallible Word of God we resist that which we ought never to resist, i.e., the truth of the miracle that here fallible men speak the Word of God in fallible human words — and we therefore resist the sovereignty of grace, in which God himself became man in Christ, to glorify himself in his humanity. . . . To the bold postulate that if their word is to be the Word of God they must be inerrant in every word, we oppose the even bolder assertion, that according to the Scriptural witness about man, which applies to them too, they can be at fault in any word, and have been at fault in every word, and yet according to the same Scriptural witness, being justified and sanctified by grace alone, they have still spoken the Word of God in their fallible and erring human word." [12]

As a result, Barth finds conservatism (and the same would apply to Catholicism) guilty of trying to possess God. Man in his sinful insecurity longs to control God. He refuses to trust God and God alone for his salvation. Instead, he claims that in the Biblical words or in his creeds he holds the very words of God himself. This is a refusal to confess that God is truly Lord and sovereign even over the Bible and revelation.[13] We can never possess God; grace alone freely gave the Bible and grace alone can cause it to be revelation to man.

The claim has been made that this view of revelation is more true to the Bible itself than the claim that revelation comes as propositional information. We do not have the space to deal adequately with this subject, but there have been a number of excellent defenses of this thesis.[14] Here we can only summarize a few points made in greater detail by other writers.

First, it is significant that the Bible is primarily a book of history. Brunner points out that it contains nothing remotely resembling a catechism or a system of doctrines.[15] There is no other sacred Scripture that provides us with such reliable and extensive historical data. John Baillie says that the Christian faith is truly " good news " because it is not a summary of eternal truths, but a report of concrete events — the things that God has done. But what is revealed through events and actions is the person of the actor. Of course, propositions must be made about the events, but such propositions point beyond themselves to the reality of what is revealed through the events.

The Biblical faith says, " I know whom I have believed " (II Tim. 1:12), not " *what* I have believed." But, as Brunner points out, the church was early overcome with an intellectualism that perverted this understanding. It switched from the personal I-thou to an impersonal I-it understanding of revelation. It changed from what Brunner calls " truth as encounter " to " truth as idea." " The church turned the revelation of the Son into the revelation of an eternal truth ' about the Son.' " [16]

Brunner, of course, recognizes as clearly as White, the Catholic, that we need doctrines and propositions to communicate the faith. Even Peter's confession, " Thou art the Christ," was a proposition. But the point is that for the believer in propositional revelation, the proposition *is* revelation, for Brunner it *points* to revelation. For the former, the proposition is beyond dispute; it must be accepted. But for Brunner, the proposition must always be kept under criticism by revelation itself. We must ask of the proposition, " Does it point to Christ? " If it does, we keep it; if not, we seek for another proposition that will do so more adequately.

The proposition, "Thou art the Christ," was the proposition that came naturally to Peter, the Jew, as he tried to express the revelation that had occurred to him in the presence of Jesus. The Christ, or Messiah, was the highest concept that a Jew had to apply to Jesus. As a witness to revelation it was necessary, but it was not inerrant, for when Peter drew the natural meaning of that time from the proposition and affirmed that Jesus should not die, Jesus rebuked him harshly (Matt. 16:21-23). Far from being an infallible statement, even to the man who spoke it, the statement had an ambiguous meaning. It is significant that the later Biblical writers seldom described Jesus as the Messiah, or Christ. Even in the New Testament the term "Christ" became a name rather than a title for Jesus. Instead, Jesus was called the Lord, the Logos (Word), the Savior, the Redeemer, the Only-begotten Son, and so on.

Sometimes these various terms to describe Jesus have been used as evidence that there are many Christologies in the New Testament. But it is my belief that such an interpretation misses the vital point. All these terms are propositions or words used to point to the revelation experienced in Christ. No one of them was adequate for the simple reason that each was a category used before Christ came, but when he came, he was unique, he belonged to no prior category. Peter quite rightly took the highest category that he knew to describe Jesus, but immediately he was shown how inadequate this category was to express the new revelation. And so other categories were tried, and each, in its own way, was an adequate pointer to the revelation, and yet each fell short. Not one could be claimed as an inerrant expression of the revelation, for any of them could be used to mean the wrong thing.[17]

And this is the problem of all creeds. They are necessary because man has to try to point to the revelation that has found him. But creeds and propositions can never be final; they must change with changing times. The church must always agonize over purity of doctrine, for doctrines are indispensable to point to Christ. If our doctrine is inadequate, it will point wrongly or dimly so that men do not see revelation. But no doctrine can be so pure that it may be placed above criticism.

Brunner says that Catholics have dogmas, Protestants have confessions of faith. Dogma is "that which one must believe"; the man who does not is excommunicated, cut off from the means of salvation. Unfortunately Protestants often have fallen into this viewpoint, but it is opposed to the genius of Protestantism. A Protestant does not believe in a doctrine; he believes in Christ. And so Luther said, "The one doctrine which I have supremely at heart, is that of faith in Christ, from whom, through whom, and unto whom all my theological thinking flows back and forth day and night." [18] Any doctrine is a confession of faith that points to Christ; it has no other purpose or value. For the Protestant the Bible and doctrine are like telescopes; they are made to look through, not to look at.

We can illustrate our position by referring to Christ. Whatever else Christians may or may not agree upon, they do agree that the fullness of God's revelation is found in him. But how is revelation found in Christ? Many have extolled Jesus as a spiritual pioneer who discovered the great spiritual truths upon which Christianity is built. This view was found in liberalism, although many liberals found it inadequate. But the problem is that Jesus was not so original a teacher as this implies. Most of Jesus' teachings find their parallels in other religions, certainly in pre-Christian Judaism.

But there is an even greater difficulty in the view of Jesus as a teacher. Brunner, building on Kierkegaard, has pointed out that Jesus fails to fulfill the essential function of a teacher. The true teacher does not point to himself; he points to the truth. He is most happy when he has made himself unnecessary, and his pupil goes forward to find the truth for himself. But if we look to the New Testament, we find that Jesus deliberately made himself indispensable; he did not point beyond himself to the truth, but he pointed to himself as "the way, the truth, and the life" (John 14:6). Jesus tells his disciples that they will be persecuted, not for his teachings, but for his "name's sake" (Mark 13:13). A man's very status before God will depend upon his relationship to Christ. "Whosoever therefore shall confess me before men, him will I confess also before my Father which is in heaven." (Matt. 10:32.) The illustrations could be multiplied to show that Jesus put himself at the center of his message.

Faced with the problem that Jesus presents himself as more than a teacher, the radical liberal often retreated to the claim that Jesus was unique because he not only taught but also lived his teachings. Although others may have taught the same things, Jesus alone lived them. Jesus is therefore important because we do not know of what man is capable until we see manhood fulfilled in Jesus. We cannot reject this view completely because Paul taught in his doctrine of the second Adam that Christ reveals what man was meant to be (Rom. 5:12-21). But precisely when we understand this, we find that we need more than a teacher and an example in Jesus, for if the perfect Christ is man as man was meant to be, we find ourselves unable to become what we were meant to be. We are sinners. And so Jesus does not simply present himself as an ideal; he calls men to himself where they may be remade by God.

Now this amazing teaching is precisely what we might expect if our view of revelation is correct. We have asserted that what the Bible reveals is the person of God. God acts, and in the Bible God inspires prophets to interpret his acts, and through this comes the revelation of God's nature, will, and person. But finally a person can be revealed fully and completely only by himself appearing. The subjects may see the acts of their king, and they may hear his messages sent through his heralds; but before they can truly know him, he must himself appear in their midst and speak with them. Therefore, if the kind of revelation to which the Bible bears witness is to be fulfilled, God himself must appear. And in Christ, the Christian believes, this mystery of mysteries has occurred. If information could have saved man, the prophets would have sufficed. But salvation requires personal communion with the Savior.

Jesus Christ is thus revelation for us, not as teacher, although we must not forget that he was a teacher, nor as example, although he was that too. Jesus becomes revelation through his whole life and person, and in them the eyes of faith see God. " God was in Christ, reconciling the world unto himself." (II Cor. 5:19.)

We can also approach the Biblical view of revelation through an analysis of the Biblical view of faith. We pointed out that if revelation is the revelation of infallible propositions, then the proper response would be to bow in submission and believe the infallible truths. Faith would thus be belief (*credentia*). In fact, it is not unusual to find defenders of this position arguing that the more unbelievable the doctrine, the greater the merit for believing it. But if we turn to the Bible, we find that saving faith does not primarily mean belief.

There are many passages on faith with which we might deal. I shall refer to the sixth chapter of Romans. Here, as elsewhere, Paul makes it clear that man is not saved by submitting his reason to divinely revealed propositions; he is saved by a faith-relationship with Christ. Shall we continue to sin so that grace can abound? asks Paul, and he answers with a resounding NO. How can we continue in sin if we have really *died* with Christ and if we now live in him alone? Where we were the slaves of sin, we have become the servants of Christ. It is quite clear that for Paul faith is not primarily a belief at all; it is a relationship with God through Christ, a relationship that remolds the whole of life.

On the other hand, if we turn to James's epistle, where salvation by faith is criticized, it is clear that James is not denying the faith that Paul is affirming. The faith that James asserts cannot save is belief in doctrine. Thus he says, " Thou believest that there is one God; thou doest well: the devils also believe, and tremble." (James 2:19.) We know that in the later writings of the New Testament, the concept of faith as belief was already beginning to form. In James we find an attack upon such a concept. But James is not in opposition to Paul. The belief that a devil can have is not the faith through which Paul found that he was a new man in Christ.

Again we admit that every act of faith in the Pauline sense will include, at least implicitly, certain beliefs. John Baillie says, " When I trust somebody . . . I am manifestly at the same time believing certain things about him to be true, yet I may find it very difficult to say exactly what these things are — I may even flounder helplessly in the attempt to assign the reasons for my trust." [19] And so the propositions believed in saving faith may be so implicit that the believer is at loss to express them. The purpose of theology is to clarify the propositions involved in faith, but we must never mis-

take belief in the propositions for the faith. There may be faith
with only implicit belief; there may be explicit belief without faith.

In the Bible we find continually the theme that we are to have
faith in God. Barth says that if we are true to the Bible, we must
meet the surprising fact that the Bible never points to itself but always to God. Conservatism runs the danger of losing this Biblical
insight. Subtly it calls us to put faith in the Bible, the inerrant book,
while Catholicism calls us to faith in the church.

The appeal to the authority of the church or Bible has its difficulties. If the unbeliever asks why he should accept the Bible as
infallible, it is hard to give a reason. We may quote the Bible itself,
but the verses are ambiguous and the argument is circular. Even if
the quoted verses do say that the Bible is infallible (and I fail to see
that they do), the man who doubts its infallibility will doubt the
verses. We cannot use the miracles to persuade the unbeliever because he doubts the truth of all miracle stories. If we say that the
Bible is an ancient book that has long inspired and guided men,
and if we point to its high moral tone, its fine style, etc., the unbeliever quite rightly points out that the same can be said for the
Bhagavad-Gita, the Analects of Confucius, and other sacred books.

But not only is the method ineffective; it is most destructive when
it is successful. Brunner points out that it puts Christianity upside
down. " It bases our faith-relation to Jesus Christ upon our faith in
the apostles." [20] That is, *because* we believe the Bible or the church,
we believe in Christ. But this is not Christian faith at all. We are
not called to believe in Christ because the Bible or some apostle
tells us to do so. We believe because God has convinced us just as
God convinced Peter. The Christian ought not first to believe in
the trustworthiness of apostle, church, or Bible. He first comes to
faith in Christ, and through this he is led to a secondary belief in
the words of the Bible, the apostle, or the church.

This viewpoint certainly has its justification in the teachings of
Luther and Calvin. But I believe that it is unfortunate that the men
who have rediscovered this in the present century have so widely ignored the witness of sectarian Christianity at this point. For it was
the Reformation sects, with their deep suspicion of all human au-

thorities, who often witnessed most clearly to the principle. We can point, for example, to George Fox. He wandered about the churches of his day seeking truth, but everywhere he went he found men pointing him to the authority of the church, or the Bible, or a creed. But Fox could find no peace there. And then one day, he recorded in his journal: " When all my hopes in . . . all men were gone, so that I had nothing outwardly to help me, nor could tell what to do, then, O then, I heard a voice which said, ' There is one, even Christ Jesus, that can speak to thy condition,' and when I heard it, my heart did leap for joy." Here we find the nature of Christian witness. What we have to confess is that Christ Jesus has spoken to our condition, that in him we have heard the Word of God. We can invite the unbeliever to look to Christ also. If he finds that Christ does speak to his condition, then he will believe in the Bible as the witness to the truth he has found. But if he does not find that Christ speaks to his condition, there is no way in which we can prove to him the truth of the Bible. Revelation is that which brings us to know God; it is God himself speaking to us. This is the truth, long obscured, that has been rediscovered in our time.

We began by saying that a new reformation theology has to have a view of revelation that does justice to the Reformation and to the modern situation. I believe that this is what the view we have outlined does. It emphasizes the objectivity of the revelation given by God and mediated to us through the Bible, and thus preserves the Reformers' emphasis upon the objectively given revelation in the Bible. And it also does justice to the Reformation principle that the Holy Spirit must witness to the objectively given revelation. It accepts wholeheartedly the findings of Biblical criticism. We are thankful that, having been shown the human and finite nature of the Bible, we are saved from an idolatry of the book. Finally, we do not have to insult the modern world's intelligence by calling it to submit its reason to authoritatively given propositions; we invite it instead to a " divine-human encounter " in which a new perspective is given from which one can behold the world.

Finally, when we see that the knowledge of God that the Christian claims is a person-to-person knowledge, it becomes evident that natural theology can contribute little to this knowledge. The natural theologian would gain knowledge about God by examining the world. But a scientific (or metaphysical) examination of the world will discover less about the person of the living God than the medical student can learn about the former personality of the cadaver he has been given to dissect. The student may draw some tentative conclusions about the character and person of his cadaver. From the remains he can deduce that this was a clean-living person who took care of himself and so on. But he can do this because there is a basis of comparison. He knows from past experience how other bodies have been affected by the character and life of the person. But when we try to gain a clue about God's person from the universe, we face the fact that we have only one universe — there is no other with which to compare it. Thus, for example, what the presence of evil in this world means about the character of the Creator we cannot say, since we have no way of knowing what another universe, constructed differently from ours, might be like. We may have great fun in second-guessing God in his creation, but we have only the wildest of speculation to go on. If the person and character of God are what we are trying to know, it must be God himself who reveals them to us. No one else has the information. "For what person knows a man's thoughts except the spirit of the man which is in him? So also no one comprehends the thoughts of God except the Spirit of God." (I Cor. 2:11, RSV.)

IV.

How Can We Know that Revelation Is Revelation?

WE HAVE DISCUSSED the reason-faith debate and defended the position of faith seeking understanding. We have examined revelation and accepted the position that what God reveals is God. The Christian faith arises where a man, confronted by God in Christ, finds that his ultimate perspective and frame of reference have been changed. We are now prepared to discuss the crucial question — How can we know that revelation is revelation? A strong point made by the rationalist is that fideism has no way of choosing between different claimants to revelation. Does not fideism put us at the mercy of the first fanatic who comes along shouting, " I have a revelation "?

The primary question about the test of revelation is this. Does man have some criterion, given to him as man, whereby he can set up a standard by which to judge revelation, or must revelation provide its own standard? The work of Karl Barth has forced us to ask the question. John Bennett says: " The one point in the thought of Karl Barth which came to make sense to me as early as 1938 was his insistence on the view that, if we seek to test Christian revelation by some standard from beyond itself, it is that standard upon which we really depend as the ultimate ground of faith and which is itself subject to no rational test." [1]

The problem is that God is the unique; he does not belong to any general class of divine beings. When a new creature is found by the biologist, he has his classes ready into which he can put it. By these criteria he decides whether it is a mammal or something else. But there is no class or category of our knowledge to which God belongs; therefore, we do not know in advance any criteria that we can apply to God. But if we cannot classify God, how can we judge revelation unless revelation itself gives us the criteria?

That this is not a new question can be seen in John Wesley, who put the dilemma clearly. Facing the question of how we can know that it is God speaking, he says, " To require a more minute and philosophical account of the manner whereby we distinguish these, and of the *criteria,* or intrinsic marks, whereby we know the voice of God, is to make a demand which can never be answered." [2] Suppose that Agrippa, the Roman, had demanded of Paul how he had known it was Christ speaking to him. Wesley says: " Can you believe the apostle himself would have once attempted to answer so idle a demand? And yet, doubtless the moment he heard that voice, he knew it was the voice of God. But *how* he knew this, who is able to explain? Perhaps neither man nor angel." [3] Finally, Wesley concludes that the believer knows because he has the direct confirmation of God's Word, but this can never be communicated to the natural man because it is known " even by spiritual senses which the natural man hath not." In short, Wesley saw very clearly that when the Word of God speaks to man it does not fit into and cannot be tested by any category that man possesses ahead of time.

Again, as Barth has taught us anew, God is the Lord, the Creator, and because he is Lord, he maintains his freedom, even in revelation. He is never at the mercy of man so that we can force him to reveal himself as we choose. We are saved by God's free grace, and a most important aspect of this grace is that God reveals himself freely where, and only where, he chooses. In revelation the initiative is always with God.

This freedom of God in revelation has a real analogy in human relations. A person has a certain freedom in that he can make decisions to reveal or not to reveal himself to other persons. Although this freedom is limited by our finiteness so that we often reveal aspects of ourselves inadvertently, nonetheless, we do have freedom about the revelation of our deepest self. If man has this limited but real freedom, how much more must this be true of God, the Lord.

In our interpersonal relations we cannot prove objectively and rationally the truth of the self that another reveals to us. We cannot get into the other's inner mind; we can know him only as he reveals himself. If he chooses to deceive us, there is no final guarantee against the deception. Our personal relations always involve trust. In impersonal relations we can get guarantees, contracts, etc., to protect ourselves. But in the intimacies of personal relations — love and friendship — we cannot have such objective guarantees. The very attempt to get them destroys the relationship. But the reward for the risk is that trust turns out to be a way of knowing. When we have trusted and loved the other, we can see that in them which others do not see, and so we are willing to put our lives in their hands even when we have no argument that would persuade a third person to do the same.

An important reason why we can never prove that the self which a John Smith reveals to us is his true self is because each John Smith is unique and we have no prior categories of John Smithness by which we can judge his revelation. If I try to judge John Smith by criteria other than those which he reveals by word and act, I am doomed to miss the truth. The evils of prejudice arise from judging individual John Smiths by the categories to which they belong rather than by their revelation of themselves. Prejudice says that since John Smith is a Negro, or a Jew, or an intellectual, or something else, therefore he must be so and so. It deduces from the category to which he belongs, instead of listening to the revelation he makes of himself, and the result is always misinformation.

Karl Barth has made the point we are discussing in terms of the a priori and a posteriori [4] ways of knowing. Barth insists that we have no a priori knowledge of God, that God is known only a posteriori. Prejudice, as we have seen, thinks a priori; it says that since John Smith is a Negro, he must be . . . But to let John Smith reveal what he really is, is a posteriori knowledge of John Smith.

A priori knowledge is knowledge that is implicit within the proposition itself, and is therefore known apart from any experience. The minute the mind sees what is implied in the statement it recognizes that the statement must be true. Mathematics, of course, forms the classic example of a priori truths. A priori knowledge is basically a matter of definition. We know a priori that a statement is true because we have agreed to use words so that it must be true. Thus when a man says that "the part is less than the whole," we know that this is true a priori. Any claim that it is not true would simply show that a man did not understand the way we use words; you would not argue with him; you would send him to the dictionary. Thus a priori truths are tautologies; there is nothing in the predicate of an a priori sentence that is not already contained in the subject. "All fathers have children" is true a priori because the subject, fathers, implies the having of children.

A posteriori knowledge, on the other hand, is knowledge that comes after experience; it is knowledge arrived at in the light of facts. In a priori thinking we reason by deduction from the premises; in a posteriori thinking we examine evidence and draw conclusions from it (induction). Deduction tells us a priori that all fathers have children, but only induction, working a posteriori, can tell us how many children the average American father has.

If we overlook this distinction, we cannot understand what Barth and those like him are saying about revelation. Barth insists that we have no a priori knowledge of God. If we are to know God, we must necessarily operate in the light of experience; we do not start with a priori truths about God; we can start only from the fact of God's making himself known. Much philosophical and theological speculation about God has operated a priori. For example, Aristotle started from the premise that God is perfect and deduced that therefore God lacks nothing, therefore he can want nothing, therefore he wills nothing, since a will expresses a want of something that one does not have. Similarly, a perfect God cannot love man who is less than perfect, for the perfect would demean itself by loving the imperfect. And obviously the perfect God cannot suffer, for he lacks no perfection. This is all good deduction, but in the light of the Christian faith, it is all false. God, the Christian believes, has revealed himself, in fact, to be quite different from each of these deductions which comes from the premise of perfection.

The man who sets up a priori standards that God must fulfill if his revelation is to be accepted is a man who refuses to accept God's Lordship. Long ago scientists discovered that nature can be known only a posteriori. No longer did one decide a priori that a heavy object must fall faster than a light one; instead we drop both and let the facts decide. Barth is arguing that our knowledge of God must likewise be a posteriori.

There are two reasons why we must use an a posteriori method of knowing God. One reason comes from philosophy and one comes from theology. So far as I know, Barth does not use the philosophical reason, but it is significant.

Modern philosophy has made it clear that while a priori truths are certain, they can tell us nothing about reality. It is true a priori that all unicorns grow horns out of their heads. Show me a unicorn that never had a horn, and I can prove by definition that you have nothing but a common horse. But for all its certainty, the a priori statement does not tell us whether unicorns exist. To decide that question we have to search the world to see if any animals fitting the definition of unicorns are to be found. Even the most illustrious of a priori disciplines — mathematics — has its certainty only so long as it is kept strictly separated from space and time. Two plus two equals four — that is certain a priori. But if we have two male plus two female rabbits, and if we allow some time to pass, the total is no longer four. The only way to find out how many rabbits will result is to use a posteriori methods.

So if a priori thinking can never tell us about existing reality, it cannot be helpful in knowing the truth about what God is. If we are to know God, we must let him speak for himself. We can only know God a posteriori, that is, where God is made known in reality. Once more we find the paradox that Barth, whom we have discarded as " irrational," is developing a method of thought that is closer than that of many philosophical theologians to reason as understood in some of the main currents in contemporary philosophy.

On the other hand, theology, working a posteriori, in the light of revelation, also gives reason why God cannot be known a priori. God as revealed is the Lord; he is completely sovereign and completely free. Where there is freedom, it is impossible to know a

priori how the free agent will act. We can never say a priori that
God has to do something. The only necessity ruling God's action is
the necessity of his own nature. But what that is we cannot know
except as God reveals it to us.

The man who tries to set up a priori criteria for revelation ends
up by dictating to God. As Barth has put it:

> "We put ourselves, so to speak, midway between God and man,
> with a twofold illusion and assumption, the claim to know what
> God can and must do, to know what is necessary and appropriate
> to us men so that revelation between him and us can become an
> event. . . . In such circumstances, it is inevitable that even the
> most conscientious theology will prescribe for God what his revela-
> tion must be and how it must be handled, if he is to count upon
> our recognition of it as such." [5]

An example of such a priori thinking is found in the conservative
theologian, E. J. Carnell. He says, "Whenever we are confronted
with doctrines or practices which outrage our sense of decency, we
can be negatively assured that they do not originate in God." [6] Actually this statement undercuts Carnell's own position. As a conservative, he holds the doctrine of substitutionary atonement —
the view that Christ died as a substitute for sinful man and, in his
death, bore the penalty of man's sin. But one of the most persistent
arguments against this doctrine has been that it outrages man's
sense of decency in having one man punished for another's sin.
Presumably it does not outrage Carnell's sense of decency, but why
should we prefer his sense of decency to that of the man who is outraged?

Barth would find Carnell's dilemma a fitting judgment upon the
presumption of setting up a priori categories for God to fulfill. Even
if the result of such categories is to prove God's revelation satisfactory, it is a small compliment to pay to God to tell him that he does
not outrage our sense of decency. But the trouble is, how can sinful
man be sure that God will not outrage his sense of decency? Perhaps it should be outraged. Only after the revelation of God has

been made can we decide how our sense of decency will fare. To make it a condition of God's revelation that he must meet any a priori categories that we set up is to refuse to accept God as God.

It may be objected that I have been guilty of a priori method earlier in this chapter. I argued that God was unique and did not fit our categories, that he was the Lord who gave himself where he willed, and I drew analogies with our knowledge of other persons. It may have seemed that these were a priori conclusions. But actually this was a posteriori reasoning. God, as revealed in Scripture, has revealed himself as unique, as Lord, as free, and as personal. Only in the light of the revelation can we argue a posteriori that such is the case.

We have reached the point where we can say that it is not irrational to argue that the only criteria by which revelation can be judged are the criteria that revelation itself gives. In fact, this is quite analogous to our relationship to nature in science. Science became effective when it quit arguing about nature a priori and studied it a posteriori, finding in nature itself the criteria by which nature was to be known.

This means that our new reformation theology can affirm the Reformation doctrine of *sola Scriptura,* that is, the doctrine that the basis of the Christian faith is the Scriptures alone. This is not to say that there is no revelation apart from Scriptures. Whether or not revelation of the true God has appeared outside of Scripture is to be decided a posteriori by looking to see whether there is faith in the true God where the Scriptures are not known. But the *sola Scriptura* principle does mean that, wherever there is a claim to revelation, the Christian must judge it by the criteria of revelation presented in Scripture itself. Man, we believe, apart from the Scriptural revelation, does not have a criteria to judge revelation. This is why Wesley desired to be a " man of one book." [7]

There are some who will shudder at what I am saying here, for it will seem to them that in making our knowledge of God a posteriori we have lost the certainty of Christianity. If modern philosophy teaches us that a priori truths tell us nothing about reality, it is equally convinced that a posteriori findings can never be certain. [8]

Thus if we have no a priori criteria to judge, we can never be certain that Christianity is true. This is quite true so far as rational certainty is concerned, and it is necessary to face and accept this situation in humility. We can never be logically certain that a friend is trustworthy or that nature will still operate lawfully tomorrow, and yet we bet our lives on both. In the same way, we have the certainty of trust in God, but to the end we walk by faith and not by sight. In fact, the desire for a certainty that would eliminate the necessity of trust is sinful because it is the desire to have God in man's power.

Kierkegaard saw clearly that reason is incapable of proving the Christian revelation to be true. Christianity is based on the claim that the Lord God, the Creator of all, became incarnate in Christ. How can such a claim be measured? It will not do to judge it by its consistency with our knowledge apart from this event. If God is truly the Creator and the Lord, then his entry into human life must be paradoxical, and it must transcend our rational understanding. If it does not strain to the breaking point our rational understanding, we could not really believe that this was God. So, if God is truly present in Christ, we have no way to test for his presence analogous to testing for chlorine in our water supply. We have no class of incarnations into which we can fit Jesus to test his claim.

If we try to prove the Christian faith by the miracles of Jesus, we immediately see that other religions also claim miracles; and if miracles prove the divinity of Jesus, why don't they prove the divinity of Buddha? Sometimes we try to prove the truth of Jesus' divinity by pointing to his profound ethical insights and his high moral life. But this is no evidence of divinity. For one thing, the enthusiasm for Jesus' ethics is always in part due to being raised in a Christian culture. To the man trained in another culture, with different ethical ideals, Jesus' ethics, like the value he gave to the person of man or his teaching about forgiveness, are seen as an argument against his divinity. But even if we should decide that Jesus' ethical teachings are by all odds the most profound, it would prove nothing more than that he was an ethical genius.

We face the same problem if we approach Christianity with mankind's best thoughts on the nature of God. If we judge Christ's teaching and life in terms of what we already know about God, what could we prove? In so far as there was a correlation between Christ and our prior knowledge of God, it would only prove that Christ had the knowledge of God that other men have. Only in so far as he represented new insights about God could he be a new revelation. But, of course, it would be precisely the truth of this new revelation that our old knowledge of God could not confirm.

Even the negative test here cannot be decisive. If Christ should violate our best moral thinking and our best thought about God, what would it prove? It might prove that Christ was a false prophet, but it could equally well prove that our best thinking on these matters had been distorted and was in urgent need of revision. The greatest moral philosophers of Greece, for example, would have been shocked at Jesus' teaching about the equality of man and the preference to be given to the poor and weak. Today most Christians would say that they needed to be shocked at these points. But can we be sure that our own ethical ideals are not equally in need of being shocked? In short, faced with the claim that God has appeared in our midst incarnate, we are unable to suppose that we have enough prior knowledge of God to judge the truth of this claim. Such a claim puts a demand upon us for a decision. It is a challenge to the faith presupposition by which we live. But this means that it is a challenge to the very frame of reference within which we would judge it.

It is difficult to find an adequate analogy for what is involved here. But if there is such an analogy, it must come from personal relationships. Perhaps there is an analogy in the relationship of love. In a love relationship the question often is asked, " Why do you love me? " If a man answered his wife or sweetheart with, " Because you perform such miracles in your cooking," she would be quite justified in crowning him with a frying pan. But it would be no better if he answered that it was because she made such profound moral judgments or because she had such a brilliant mind. In that case she would live in suspense lest she make a wrong moral judgment or appear stupid and thus lose his love. In the last analysis, there is only one adequate answer; it is simply, "I love you because you are you." Of course, this includes the cooking ability, the moral judgments, and the wisdom, but it does not leave the love at the mercy of any of these. It means that the loved one makes a total impact upon the lover, so that his only possible response is that of love.

Similarly, when the Christian confesses faith that Christ is God incarnate, he can only answer "Why?" by saying, "Because Jesus is Jesus." The total impact that he makes upon us is such that we can only respond to him in faith. Arguments can never make us love a woman, and where we do love, no argument can destroy it. Likewise, it is important to see that no argument can create faith, and where there is true faith, no argument can destroy it. This is what Kierkegaard saw so clearly: a rational argument ends with a conclusion, but faith is not a conclusion; faith is a decision, a commitment, a response. Thus where there is faith in Christ, we can confess that it is only by grace, that is, it is not due to our efforts, but is the response won from us by the fact of Christ presented to us. As we "fall in love," so we "fall into grace." This is why the Reformers said that the Holy Spirit must witness to the truth of the Scriptural revelation.

Reason cannot prove the Christian claim to revelation, but the fact that it cannot does not lead to irrationalism. We have referred to the analogy of knowing John Smith and insisted that we have no criterion of John Smithness by which we can judge this particular John Smith apart from his revelation of himself. But it is obvious that reason is not paralyzed by this situation. We do not accept at its face value every revelation that John Smith gives of himself. If his actions belie his words, or if what he says today is inconsistent with what he said yesterday, we begin to doubt him, not because we have a source of knowing John Smith other than his revelation, but because the revelation provides its own criteria of judgment.

It is a common criticism of Kierkegaard that he had no way of discrediting a false prophet. But such critics overlook the fact that a false prophet arose in Denmark in Kierkegaard's lifetime, a minister named Adler, and Kierkegaard wrote a masterful book to show up his falseness.[9] Kierkegaard found that Adler contradicted his own claim to revelation. Some days Adler insisted that he had had a direct revelation; some days he backed down and confessed that it was not really revelation. Adler himself provided the criteria by which Adler was refuted. Similarly, the Christian does not have faith in Christ because he said that he was " the way, the truth, and the life." He has faith because he finds that Christ's total life and teaching are consistent with the claim that Jesus made for himself.

To illustrate our point we might look back to the Jews who rejected Jesus in his lifetime. Their basis for denying Jesus was that he did not fit coherently into their preconceived system of ideas about what the Messiah should be. He did not lead an army to conquer Rome, as many of them hoped. But the point is that if Jesus is truly Messiah, then it is Jesus alone who can define what Messiahship is to be. And in view of the way in which he defined Messiahship, it would be a disproof of his claims if he had led a revolt against Rome — even if he had won. The task of Christian apologetics is to show that Jesus was consistent, not with our prior concepts of God, but with his own claims for himself. Space does not permit me to perform this task, but it has been done frequently by others.[10]

The understanding that reason can examine a claim to revelation in terms of its consistency with its own criteria is our justification for Biblical criticism. A new reformation theology has more concern with Biblical criticism than did even liberalism. Just because we believe that God is revealed through the Bible, it becomes the more necessary to be critical of the Bible. We must be careful to separate the wheat from the chaff precisely because we believe that from the wheat is formed the bread of life.

At first sight the conservative's willingness to accept the words of the Bible as the inerrant revelation of God seems to be a higher faith and a more worthy trust than that of the Biblical critic. But if every word of the Bible is not a word of God, then it is blasphemy to charge God with speaking all of them. Thus it is not a lack of faith that causes me to deny that God ordered Saul to slaughter his enemies to the last woman and child (I Sam. 15:2-3) or that he sent bears to eat children who laughed at a prophet's bald head (II Kings 2:23-25). On the contrary, it is my faith in God through Christ that forces me to deny this. It is not that my moral sensitivity is outraged by such stories, although it is, but then my moral sensitivity may be most unlike that of God, whose ways are not my ways. But I deny these stories because in Christ, I believe, revelation itself gives us the criteria by which we can judge. If Christ is God incarnate, then all revelation must be judged by this final revelation. Jesus himself contradicted Biblical teachings, and thereby he gives us the right to do the same, assuming that it is done in light of his revelation. (Matt. 5:38-39, 43-44.)

In other words, it seems to me that conservatism is guilty of a priori thinking on revelation. It starts with the claim that the perfect God must give a perfect revelation, and deduces that the Bible must be without error. But if we humbly submit to a posteriori thinking, we shall not dictate to God how he must reveal himself in the Bible, but examine the facts and see how he has done so.

Despite the fact that we see no possibility of a criterion apart from revelation by which revelation may be judged, this does not leave us at the mercy of the first fanatic to come along. We have every right to test, by reason, any claim to revelation in terms of its correlation with its own claim. As an actual matter of fact, this presents us with the sufficient argument against most fraudulent claims to revelation. Sooner or later the would-be prophet contradicts his own claim. His teaching or his life fails to meet his own criteria. Although we have made no pretense at proving that Christianity meets this criteria, we have tried to indicate the lines along which this can be demonstrated. Of course, it is possible, in principle, for a claim to revelation to be perfectly consistent with itself and still be false. But any claim to revelation must satisfy its own criteria before it can be taken seriously.

The Biblical revelation sets forward an important criterion. It is found in the Old Testament's battle against idolatry. The significance of this battle is that we are called to worship the God who created us, not the gods that we create. As Karl Barth has told us frequently, religion consists in man's creating his own gods and idols, and even the Christian religion has been guilty of this. When man creates idols, he makes his gods into the kind of beings that he wants to worship and to serve. To believe in the God of Scripture, the Creator and Lord of all, is to set our faces firmly against every item of wishful thinking in religion.

The battle against idolatry has become more subtle since the days of the prophets, but it has not become any less urgent. People in Christian countries have no graven images in their rooms, but they have them in their hearts. Sometimes idolatry takes crude forms, as in the popular god of American folk religion, "the man upstairs," who will give health, wealth, and success to all who perform the proper acts and repeat the prescribed verses of Scripture. But sometimes idolatry is more respectable, as when a clever philosopher or theologian offers for worship a metaphysical god. But wherever it appears, idolatry offers a god of human invention, a god that man would like to have and believe in, a god that blesses us as we are and promises us those things which our hearts already desire. All too frequently such a god is identified with the Biblical God.

The claim that we are to worship the God who created us justifies the demand to listen to reality first instead of thinking about God a priori. A priori thinking is an excellent device for preserving idolatry. Any God produced from out of man's mind is likely to be an idol. The God who created us must reveal himself to us or we will not know him. The many forms of existentialism that are being used in theology today need to be watched closely at this point, since, beginning with an existential analysis of man's condition, they are in grave danger of ending up with a god cut to meet man's need.

This principle has much in common with our Western admiration for the disinterested search for truth. In fact, we can, from a Christian perspective, understand the unbeliever's desire for truth as a hunger for God. He is expressing the restlessness that Augustine found in every man's heart until he found his rest in God. We can go farther; we can say that the atheist who, in the name of truth, refuses to accept the popular and comfortable views of deity that are presented to him, is actually closer to the true God than the man who blindly swallows the comfortable dogmas that he wants to believe. As Will Herberg has shown brilliantly, Freud's claim that religion is an illusion based on wishful thinking is actually closer to the Biblical position than that of those modern psychiatrists who argue that we should give men comfortable religious beliefs to fit their psychological needs.[11]

This principle, explicitly put before us in the Bible, refutes the idea that faith destroys critical thinking. In a real sense, it is the beginning. Who will test all theories more critically than the man who has been called to worship the true God and who knows something of the idolatrous tendencies of man, including himself? Luther warned us that man will always worship and that if he does not worship God, he will worship the devil. But, as Luther makes clear in his commentary on Galatians, the most popular way to worship the devil is to call him God. The believer is not, as modern myth pictures him, a man who has quit thinking and refuses to examine his own position. On the contrary, he is one who has been so captured by the desire for truth that he will continually be critical of all conclusions, including his own.

This explains the seriousness with which Barth accepts the criticism of the atheist Feuerbach. Feuerbach argued that God is simply man's projection of himself into the heavens. And Barth finds that this is true of man's religion. Only when we renounce this god of our own projection can we be open to the true God, the living Lord who confronts us in revelation. It is at this point that I appreciate deeply analytic philosophy, even the logical positivists. These men have stripped our idols from us; they bring out the nonsense of the gods that religion and metaphysics continually create. But when we have come face to face with the living God, we can accept these criticisms with thanksgiving. What Christianity criticizes in such men is not that they are critical; the trouble is that they are not sufficiently critical of their own faith.

The religious history of man is summed up in the story of Mt. Sinai (Ex., chs. 31; 32). The God who created man called Moses up into the mountain to receive his revelation and commandments. But at the foot of the mountain the believers in do-it-yourself religion got to work. "We do not need to go up to the mountain where God reveals himself," they argued; "we can know God anywhere or any-time that we put our minds to it." And so they created their own god — the golden calf. The golden calves are the gods men want: the tame gods that are always on our side, ready to bless us with everything that we desire. But the God hidden in the clouds on Sinai is a demanding God; he has his own will for us, and so we reject him for the pleasant gods of our own devising.

Fear of idolatry should not force us into a masochistic position where we reject every thought that gives us any happiness. But it should cause us to be suspicious of any position that fulfills all our heart's desires. When the Christian faith is made into a sweetness-and-light promise, as it is in so much popular religious literature today, we must be suspicious of it. The Bible never offered us free-dom from worry, simple peace of mind, a heaven without a hell, a God who is always on our side, who will assure us of the kind of health, success, and popularity that our sinful hearts desire. And when a religion comes offering these, we can know that we are face to face with the same problem of idolatry that the prophets faced.

There is another criterion implied within Biblical revelation it-self. It is the promise that, as the Quakers put it, the Word of God will "speak to our condition." In other words, the Bible claims to enlighten us about our situation — why we are here and what our nature and purpose is. Taken by itself, the demand that a religion speak to our condition is dangerous. That is why I mention it only after insisting upon the criterion against idolatry. Until we have been warned of our tendencies to create the gods that we want, we are unable to see the true meaning of a revelation that speaks to our condition. In our natural state we think that a religion speaks to our condition, when it offers us what we already desire.

Martin Luther is a good example of what I am trying to say here. When Luther first discovered the Biblical teaching of salvation by grace, it was not what he wanted at all. He wanted a hold upon God; he wanted to be so righteous that God would have to accept him. But Luther found that the Bible told him he could never be that good. In fact, he could never have any claim upon God. He had to trust God's goodness without assurance or proofs. Instead of being assured of God's favor toward him, he had to be prepared to be damned for the sake of God. Instead of proving that he had done enough good works to please God, the Bible told Luther that he was a sinner who could never please him, that when he had done all, he was to count himself as still an unworthy servant.

The Biblical message did not speak to Luther's condition in the sense of promising Luther what he already wanted or of telling him what he already knew. But, as Luther examined his life in the perspective of the Biblical teaching, he was forced to admit its truth. His works were not good enough to earn God's reward; he was lost in sin. And when he surrendered himself to the Biblical teaching, he found that his needs were met, not in the way in which he had asked to have them met, but in a way that removed his former requests. When Luther stood before the Diet of Worms, proclaiming that here he stood because he could do no other, he was simply witnessing to the fact that in his life and experience the Christian faith had spoken truly. Its truth had not been pleasant or desirable from his pre-Christian point of view, but it had been compelling.

In our discussion of faith and reason we said that a faith is held because of its ability to illuminate life as it is lived. The Christian affirms the Biblical revelation because, when he views the facts of life from that perspective, they take on a meaning and a significance that they do not have from any other perspective. Reinhold Niebuhr has been a highly effective apologist for the Christian faith by demonstrating how the Christian perspective interprets the facts and events of our century more adequately than any of its rivals. He has shown that, whether or not we like it, it does speak to our condition.

We are not saying that to speak to our condition a revelation must be one that we could have concluded from the facts of life; nor do we say that it must fit into our prior knowledge with logical coherence. On the contrary, such a claim to revelation would be highly suspect. Since it would offer no more than we could find out for ourselves, it would only be brilliant insight.

It is significant that the scientific views of the Bible are obviously the scientific views of the age in which the Bible was written and thus out of harmony with the scientific views of today. This has disturbed many Christians who keep producing unconvincing arguments to show that Biblical science and modern science can be reconciled. But instead of being embarrassed, the Christian ought to rejoice. Science is something that man can discover for himself; there is no reason why it should be revealed to him. The Bible has not lived because it has told man what he could discover for himself. It has lived because it reveals God's will and person. It reveals man's true nature and ultimate destiny. It makes possible the divine-human fellowship; it mediates the power that redeems and re-makes lives. In short, it has lived because it has told man what he could not, in the nature of the case, have learned from any analysis of the world. It has given him the perspective from which he could understand the world, not new information about the world.

There is a final criterion of revelation that revelation itself supplies. A claim to revelation is rationally tested by its ability to fulfill its own promises. This is a point that makes it clear why we cannot judge a claim to revelation by standards that we have apart from revelation. If we have set up our own goals in life, if we know what we want out of life, then we will judge a revelation in terms of how it satisfies our desires. It is a poor attempt at apologetics to argue that we must be Christian to save American democracy, or to bring world peace, or to give peace to our troubled mind, or to protect us from the anxieties that beset us. In such an apologetic, Christianity is made into high-class voodooism from which we can get everything that we wanted before we became Christian. But Christianity does not stand or fall upon its ability to save American democracy or to do anything else that we want. It can be judged only in terms of whether or not it redeems its own promises. And in this context we must recall that one of the promises that Jesus made was that his followers could expect persecution, suffering, and the bearing of a cross (John 15:20; Mark 8:34-35).

No claim to revelation can be judged in terms of whether it supplies what we already want. That still leaves us at the level of worshiping the gods of our own creation. The Christian faith makes some concrete promises, and one reason why men have been convinced of the truth of Christianity is that they have found its promises redeemed in their lives. They found no simple peace of mind, but they found a peace that passes understanding. (It passes understanding because it is not the peace for which the unbeliever thinks that he is seeking.) They found no protection from misfortune: the rain continued to fall on believer and unbeliever alike, but they have found that in the midst of misfortune they have walked with God (Rom., ch. 8). Here is a concrete test of revelation that does not rest upon any a priori dictating to God of what he must do. It lets God set up his own criteria and then tests them by the living of life in faith.

Perhaps the center of the Christian promise is the gift of the Holy Spirit. (Luke 11:13; John 14:26.) Here the experience of the believer and the objectivity of the given revelation come together. This is why Luther said that only God can tell you that this is God speaking. The Bible and experience come to stand together because the Bible promises the experience and the experience is held under the objective criteria of the Bible. Together they assure us that this is the Word of God spoken to man.

We have argued that in the nature of the case it would be irrational to expect to have criteria by which we could judge a revelation from God. The revelation must provide its own criteria of judgment. Christian faith is not a conclusion from a rational analysis of the universe but is a basic commitment of the self in response to the self-authenticating nature of the revelation claim. But we have tried to show that there is nothing irrational about this. On the contrary, with the coming of faith, reasoning does not end, but it begins, for it obtains a new perspective from which it can see reality. If we believed that revelation consisted of certain informational propositions, and if we claimed that there could be no test for them apart from revelation, it would be irrational. The mind would have to swallow the propositions and refuse to question further. We would be in the position of Alice's Queen, who could sometimes believe six impossible things before breakfast. But if what is revealed is God himself, and if in the very act of revelation we are involved in a personal relationship with God that throws a new light upon our whole existence, then it does not mean any abandonment of reason.

Furthermore, what is given in revelation is not a series of conclusions that shut off all further thought; instead, there is given an ultimate perspective. Thought begins in the light of this perspective in order that the faith may find understanding. The faith is justified by the ability of its perspective to illuminate the whole of life. Reason, as we have argued, always operates within the framework of some faith-perspective. If we do not accept the Christian perspective, we will not be without a perspective, but we will have another one. But it is no more possible to prove this perspective than it is to prove the Christian faith. Every man lives by faith in the perspective that has convinced him.

∵

In the last three chapters we have been developing a methodology for a new reformation theology. In the debate about reason and faith we have chosen the position of faith seeking understanding. It is not a case of reason versus faith; nor is it a question of the co-operation of two separate methods. It is the recognition that in any living situation the two are always intertwined. God is known by the faith-reason act in the light of God's revelation of himself. God does not reveal propositions about himself, but he reveals himself to man through history. This revelation arouses faith; it transforms a man's basic frame of reference. This faith seeks understanding that results in propositions about God, theology, creeds, etc. God's revelation cannot be proved apart from faith; it can only be accepted or rejected. When Christ stands at the door of our hearts, he knocks; he does not use a battering ram to break in. Man must make a choice. But God does not ask for a "blind" faith; the revelation does have its own witness to itself; it brings its own criteria of verification.

I have asserted that faith includes both an element of *fides* (cognition) and *fiducia* (trust). If either is lacking, it is not the Christian faith. When I trust a person, I do not usually perform a blind act of trusting. I do not trust all persons; why, then, do I trust some? Here reasons are complex and vary greatly from case to case. But, to generalize briefly, I " size up " the person in terms of the total impact that he has made upon me before I commit myself in trust toward him. In any act of trusting another there is, in addition to the commitment of trust, a cognitive act in which the one trusting has judged the other worthy of trust. Of course, like all cognitive acts, it is fallible and may be mistaken. But it is seldom that we trust if there is no such element involved. It is this primitive cognitive act which I would call *fides.*

But this cognitive act of *fides* is not to be identified with belief. Beliefs arise only as the *fides* seeks understanding. Some beliefs are no doubt implicit in any act of *fides* that leads to trusting, but they are often not consciously held. It is only if someone asks, " Why are you disposed to trust this person? " that the *fides* moves toward understanding and formulates its belief. And we know that often we can say little more than " I trust him because he seems to be trustworthy." Certainly the child has trusted his mother for a long time before he performs a rational act of believing something about her. This is a sketchy summary of the act of trusting, but I believe that anyone who analyzes it more fully will see that there is an underlying act of " knowing " the person that predisposes us to act trustingly toward him. Similarly we are arguing that the Christian faith in God as trust is preceded by a cognitive relationship with God.

It is always dangerous when speaking about Christian faith to move away from personal analogies, for Christian faith is a person-to-person relationship. But we may find an analogy in our knowledge of the external world. We have sensory perceptions, but sensory perceptions are not knowledge. I do not see globs of color before me or feel hardness; I see pens, paper, and an ink bottle, and I feel the keys of a typewriter. That is, every act of cognition involves an interpretation of sense impressions. The kind of interpretation involved in my illustration consists primarily of putting my sense impressions into categories suggested by my past experience. These interpretations are beliefs about the external world, and after I have tested them to my satisfaction I say that I know them.

But, although we are not aware of it, the interpretation of sense data begins long before I articulate beliefs about this or that object within my world. My sense data stir within me a sense of finding "significance," as John Hick calls it.[12] That is, my experience of the world impresses me with the fact that it has significance for me, it is meaningful to me, I can know it. I interpret my experience to be the experience of a real world outside my mind. If Hume is right, and I believe that he is, we accept the reality of a continuing physical universe, the principle of causality within it, and the continuity of the self, with what Hume calls a "natural belief." That is, these matters cannot be proved by reason. The philosopher has no more reason for accepting them than the simple man-on-the-street.

Before we begin to formulate beliefs about the world, we have already reacted to it in terms of the basic attitudes of accepting its reality, interpreting it in terms of causality, seeing that it has significance or meaning for us and so on. It is this basic reaction to the world which I would call *fides*. It is a cognitive act, but it is not the conclusion of any reasoning process; on the contrary, it is the beginning for all reasoning processes about the world. Because of the impact of the world upon him, a man commits himself in trust to it. The whole venture of science is based upon trust in the reliability of the order of nature. Most of us are not aware of deciding to accept this *fides* about the world, but if we meet a man who insists that all our sensory data are illusions, we become aware that we have no reasons that can persuade him. Johnson tried kicking a rock to refute what he interpreted as such a position, but although it may have given him great psychological satisfaction, it proved nothing except that Johnson had the "illusion" of having a toe that had a pain in it. If the Hindu says that it is all maya, or illusion, or if a Christian Scientist tells us that it is the perversion due to "mortal mind," or if an idealist philosopher tells us that it is a thought in the mind of the Absolute, we can only answer that our *fides* is different from his, that we have chosen to commit ourselves in a way that he has not. In short, all our thinking about the world that we experience begins from a basic *fides* that seeks understanding. And it seeks it because we have committed ourselves to some form of trust in our experience.

It is our thesis that our recognition of God is a basic *fides* reaction to an impact made upon us. In Christ the Christian finds the impact of the divine upon him. He has *fides* in Christ in the sense that he has a cognitive relationship to Christ. This is to put in philosophical language something of what the Christian means when he says that the Holy Spirit witnesses to the reality of God in Christ Like our *fides* in the external world, this *fides* seeks understanding and thus forms beliefs about God, man, and Christ. But faith is not belief on poor evidence; it is the cognitive relation from which thinking begins, the perspective in the light of which we think, not a conclusion that we reach.

The statement, " Christ is Lord," sounds at first like a conclusion, so that we want to know what evidence leads to it. But this statement is not a conclusion from something else; this describes a basic orientation toward life and the world. The man who has the faith that Christ is Lord is a man who sees all things in terms of Christ's Lordship. Because he believes Christ is Lord, he will have a different evaluation of the significance of all events and facts. This is not a conclusion from facts; this is a frame of reference that selects, evaluates, and weighs the facts. It is not a metaphysical statement about some other world or life; it is a way of looking at and living in this life and world.

This interpretation of faith and reason, which has been slowly emerging in recent thought, both philosophical and theological, has many important implications. For one thing, it means a complete reversal of traditional apologetics. Since Aquinas, Christian apologetics have proceeded on the assumption that it was the duty of reason, unaided by the faith, to examine the world and to construct a rational argument that would lead to God as its conclusion. But the history of apologetics is interesting. First of all, they have always been held in suspicion by Christians, for the apologist often perverts the faith in his zeal to prove it. What he proves does not turn out to be Christianity. The danger, however, seemed to be a risk worth taking if some could be won to the gospel. But increasingly the philosophical world has discredited the procedures of apologetics. Through Hume, Kant, and the analytic philosophers of today, the traditional apologetics have been demonstrated to lack logical persuasion. They may comfort the believer, but they do not change the skeptic. Whether or not we like it, we have to confess that today Christianity has no rational proofs in this sense.

This has been a difficult conclusion for many Christians to face, and so they have continued to write apologetics even though no one but fellow Christians read them. Other Christians, however, have welcomed the situation as a way to free the purity of the gospel from the inroads of alien philosophies. With Paul they have been happy to ignore the wisdom of men and to preach Christ crucified. But neither group has fully understood the implications of the new situation. This is probably the next great problem for theology to face, and, in facing it, there may come a completely new period in the relationship of philosophy and theology.

I certainly do not have the space to perform this theological task in this book. But I would like to point to the direction that seems to be appearing. The older apologetics always worked on the assumption that the Christian faith, belief in God, etc., were conclusions to be arrived at. But our new insights are forcing us to realize that Christian *fides* is not at the end of a rational argument; it is at the beginning or not at all. Every rational discussion of Christianity begins either with the faith or without it. Fortunately or unfortunately, as the case may be, we cannot distinguish between those who approach the question with a "bias" and those who do not. At best we can only ask what the "bias" is and how does it operate. The apologist can rationally persuade only those who begin from the same faith-perspective as he.

Traditional apologetics always implied that the question, Is there a God? was analogous to the question, Are there cookies in the jar in the cupboard? Both questions ask for conclusions to be arrived at by the appropriate methods of investigation, and the task of the apologist is to find the appropriate methods of investigating God's existence. But cookies are objects that can be classified, and we have methods at hand for investigating such objects. The Christian God, however, is unique; he is not another object within the world of objects. And so apologetics always runs the danger of turning God into an object.

But if our analysis of faith is correct, the question about God is nothing like that about the cookies. In the case of the cookies we know how to operate: We go to the cupboard and, opening the jar, find objects that look like cookies. If we still doubt, we eat one to see if it tastes like cookies. And if we have a really hardy skeptic in our midst, we may have a chemical analysis made. Normally this would settle the question. But suppose someone declared that he could not trust the verdict of the senses. Sensory data are all illusions; the sight, taste, and chemical composition of the objects still fail to prove that there are cookies in the jar or that there is even a jar and a cupboard. They are just a further collection of insignificant illusions. As analytic philosophers, we might tell the skeptic he was talking meaningless nonsense; we might go on eating the cookies and tell him what he was missing; we might quit talking to him. But we could not persuade him. We could not prove the existence of cookies to him because what we call proof in such cases is a method that we have worked out in the light of our *fides* that our sensory data give us significant knowledge. But where that *fides* is denied there can be no proof, because the presuppositions of proof are lacking.

God's existence and the truth of Christianity are not parallel to the question of cookies in the cupboard but to the *fides* we have in our experience of the external world. A man does not believe in God because a fine argument has been presented to him. Even where he is persuaded by such an argument, it does not necessarily result in faith. The Christian believes in God because he believes that he has actually encountered God, known God, talked with God, existed in an I-thou relationship with God. He witnesses that he has met God in prayer, in worship, in the church, in the pages of the Bible, but primarily in the person of Christ.

It is impossible to prove the reality of the objective world, because what we call proof is an operation based on the assumption of the reality and the significance of the objective world. It is not only impossible to prove the reality of the objective world, but it is also nonsensical to ask about it, for we have no criteria by which we can test its reality. No conceivable state of affairs can count for or against the statement that the observable world exists. If I go to the cupboard and see, feel, and taste the cookies, then they exist in the only sense in which we can use the term " exist." In the same way it is impossible to prove God's existence; here too there is no higher criteria by which we can decide. But as the objective world makes an impact upon us to which we respond by trusting its reality and significance, so God makes an impact upon us in his revelation to which we respond by trusting him. This is why J. C. Smart says that the question of God's existence no longer arises for the believer.

We find a similar situation in our ethical life. We can verify ethical statements, assuming that we are agreed upon some basic ethical values. But if we should meet a man who has had no experience of obligation, ought, duty, etc., there is no way in which we can verify to him an ethical statement. If a man asks what is his duty, we can answer his question. But if he asks, " What makes you think that I have any duties or obligations at all? " we cannot answer him. It is obviously ridiculous to tell him that he *ought* to feel an ought, that he has an obligation to feel obliged, and yet there is nothing much more that you can tell him. If his experience has produced no sense of obligation or duty, reason is powerless. There is no logical path from an indicative statement to an " ought " statement. If a man has the sense of obligation to help his fellow men in need, I can verify the statement that he ought to help John Smith by proving that John Smith is in need. But if he has no such sense of obligation, then my proof that John Smith is in need is just another interesting fact about the universe to him.

Verifying statements about God is not analogous to verifying statements within a system of ethical convictions. It is, rather, analogous to trying to prove to a man that he ought to feel an ought. That is, it is something that reason cannot achieve; only the impact of life's experience can do it.

If this analysis of our knowledge of God is correct, it has some important consequences for theology and the practice of the church. Knowledge of God is not something that we can pass from man to man as we impart the knowledge of the multiplication table or the atomic weight of uranium. The church is not the keeper of a set of infallible propositions that it must force down men's throats under the threat of hell-fire if they disbelieve. But neither is the church a battalion of philosophers who have in their possession a set of highly persuasive arguments that will outargue every doubter. The church has been left with one possession only — a gospel to proclaim.

In its evangelical work, the church has one primary task — to confront the unbeliever with the claims of God in Christ. And this means that it must tell the Christian story — the historical events on which the faith is built. It tries to witness how this gospel has given understanding and power for life. It invites the unbeliever to consider these claims, or it challenges the unbeliever to listen, to face the fact that a claim has been made upon his life. But the church can do no more than that; it must leave the unbeliever alone with his God to make his final decision. If God in Christ cannot persuade him, we surely cannot with our fine arguments or our eloquent preaching. And any attempt to frighten or cajole him into acceptance is irrelevant to the purpose of the church.

The sin of the church is always that it puts its faith in itself and not in God. Protestants love to point out this failing in Roman Catholicism, but they usually miss the same sin in themselves. We are determined to bring men into the Kingdom even if we have to drag them in kicking and screaming. We plan enticing programs to entertain them; we embrace the latest advertising methods from Madison Avenue; we construct complex metaphysical arguments; we claim to have the irreducible minimum set of propositions in our creeds; we promise them success in their business; we frighten them about hell, anxiety, or atomic destruction. We do almost anything but what we have been commissioned by God to do — proclaim the gospel and leave each man free to say yes or no.

As Matthew reports the last words of Jesus to his disciples, they were commanded to go into all the world, baptizing, and teaching what had come from Jesus, that is, they were to witness to what God had done. And how could this succeed? Jesus answers, "Lo, I am with you alway." (Matt. 28:20.) The church has one great hidden weapon: Christ is with it always. Whenever the church puts its faith in anything other than the power of the indwelling Christ, it starts again a religious revival at the foot of the mountain where a new golden calf is fashioned.

V.

God's Immanence and Transcendence

THE NATURE of God's transcendence and immanence has been one of the central theological questions of our century. No issue was more central to the fundamentalist-liberal controversy. Liberals based their theology on the conviction that God is immanent in his world. The key to fundamentalism was its supernaturalistic emphasis upon the transcendence of God. "Neo-orthodoxy" has affirmed that it has rediscovered the transcendence, or "otherness," of God.

This debate has been deeply affected by the fact that it has taken place in a world in which secular thinking has become more and more "naturalistic." Naturalisms vary and a definition covering all of them is difficult. But, generally speaking, naturalism believes that the space-time universe, all of which is *in principle* knowable to science, is a self-contained unit. Therefore, satisfactory explanations can be given for all events, *in principle,* without reference to any force, power, being, or intelligence beyond the space-time system.

I have stressed the words "in principle" because it is only fair to point out that naturalists do not claim that science has explained all aspects of the universe. It is no answer to naturalism to show that we are at present ignorant of many aspects of the universe. The naturalist admits this but argues that the only way to remove such ignorance is through further scientific investigation.

Naturalism has gained strength with the rise of natural science. But this should not be interpreted to mean that science proves naturalism. The naturalist sees each new triumph of science as a vindication of his faith, but no science can prove that there is nothing beyond scientific explanation. The scientific method is geared to understand the space-time universe; it ignores everything that cannot be manipulated empirically. As a result, it is hardly surprising that science never discovers a " nonnatural " fact.

Naturalism is no simple product of scientific thinking; it is a basic *fides* that existed long before the rise of natural science. But in an age that is fascinated with the triumphs of science, naturalism has seemed a most congenial interpretation of reality. Naturalism has also seemed more plausible in a culture that puts its highest evaluation upon material wealth, physical comfort, military power, and physical pleasures, as our culture has been doing for some time.

Supernaturalism, which has been historically associated with religion, is more difficult to define than is naturalism. Naturalism presents a picture of what John Hick calls a " bungaloid " universe, that is, a universe of one story. Supernaturalism has a picture of a " two-story " universe. Judaeo-Christian supernaturalism has specifically affirmed that the space-time universe is the creation of a God who transcends the universe. This Creator-God, without whom there would be no universe, maintains the universe in being and acts within it both by his providential guidance and through miraculous intervention.

We might sum up the difference between these two views by saying that naturalism sees a closed universe. Space time bears within itself the only possibilities for the future. These possibilities may be far more complex than we can imagine today, but they exhaust the potentialities of the universe. The supernaturalist believes in an open universe. Because God transcends the universe, there are no natural limits to what may occur. The naturalist is haunted with the dream that if only he had sufficient knowledge of the present, he could predict exactly everything that was going to happen in nature or history. The supernaturalist knows not what the future holds; he knows only who holds the future.

The contemporary discussion about transcendence and immanence in theology is beset with confusion. It is difficult to find any theologian who does not affirm both the transcendence and the immanence of God. However, theologians frequently fail to satisfy their critics that they have been true to both aspects. Thus the conservative C. Van Til, in his book *The New Modernism,* charges that Barth and Brunner both retain the immanence of liberal theology because they do not accept the temporal creation of the world as related in Genesis. But Barth would charge that a conservative like Carnell falls into immanence of the liberal variety when he says that we should not accept anything as revelation if it outrages our sense of decency. Finally, Barth and Brunner have charged each other with losing either the transcendence or the immanence of God. In part, such debates are due to a failure to understand each other's positions, but largely they are due to different meanings of immanence and transcendence.

The Bible does not have any philosophical doctrine about the relationship of God to the world, but it teaches both his transcendence and his immanence. The transcendence of God is emphasized most crucially in the doctrine of creation. God is not the *élan vital* of the world process; he is not to be identified with any aspect of the world; he is its creator. Furthermore, God does not create, as did Plato's God, from the pre-existing matter and ideas. The doctrine of creation out of nothing may not be explicitly taught in the Bible, but it is definitely implied. God is the Lord and sovereign over all that is; he is in complete control. If man has freedom to defy God's will, it is a freedom that he has only by God's willingness to grant it, and even man's freedom is limited by God's ultimate rule. Biblical eschatology thus sees the complete victory of the Creator assured.

God's transcendence is also expressed in the Biblical attack upon idolatry. Wherever man tries to make an image of God, wherever he identifies the divine with an aspect of the world, he is denying the true Lord. In pantheism God is identified with the world, and the world, or aspects within it, is worshiped as sacred. But for the Bible, only God is to be worshiped, only God is sacred. The world is good because God created it, but it is not sacred.

An extreme transcendence would see God and the world completely separated. Deism came close to this position. Its God created the world, but from then on the world operated on its own laws and God did not interfere with it. As a watchmaker makes a watch, winds it, and then allows it to run, so God made the world. But the Bible never pictures God's transcendence this way. The Biblical God is deeply concerned with his world, and he expresses this concern through his continual activity in the world. Paul could go so far toward pantheism as to say that "we live, and move, and have our being" in God (Acts 17:28). Jesus emphasizes the immanent providence of God when he asserts that the hairs of our head are numbered and that no sparrow falls without God knowing it (Matt. 10:29-30). Furthermore, God's immanent activity is central to the whole Biblical concept of revelation. God acts in history, choosing the Jews, delivering them from Egypt, sending them into exile, and bringing them back from it. Finally, the Christian believes, God culminated his historical revelation by becoming incarnate in Jesus Christ.

It is no wonder that responsible Christian thinkers hesitate to deny either the transcendence or the immanence of God. Both are too obviously central to the Biblical religion. To see the issues that do divide theologians, we can begin with looking at the fundamentalist-liberal controversy.

Fundamentalism held an uncompromising supernaturalism. The fundamentalist had no desire to deny God's immanent providence, but he saw two separate worlds, God's and man's. When God acted immediately within the world, the result was a miracle, an event without any possible scientific explanation. God had so acted in creation, and when he again acted with his creative power, a miracle was the result.[1] This is why miracles are so important to the fundamentalist. For him a miracle is the necessary sign that the transcendent God is making a revelation of himself. Without miracles there could be no special revelation. The conservative, Carnell, seems to hold the same position when he says that miracles are a *sine qua non* of special revelation. One test that any man who claims to bring a revelation should be able to pass is that he prove himself able to perform miracles.[2]

J. G. Machen summarizes the conservative conviction when he says:

" The issue does not concern individual miracles, even so important a miracle as the virgin birth. It really concerns all miracles. And the question concerning all miracles is simply the question of the acceptance or rejection of the Savior that the New Testament presents. Reject the miracles and you have in Jesus the fairest flower of humanity. . . . Accept the miracles, and you have a Savior who came voluntarily into this world for our salvation. . . . The difference between these two views is the difference between two totally diverse religions." [3]

The logic is clear. Since God and the world are essentially separated, God's immediate activity in the world must take the form of miracle. Only if there is a miracle can we know that God is at work. But where there is a miracle, there can be no scientific or natural explanation of the event. Therefore, where a natural explanation is present, the divine significance of the event is doubtful.

This logic led the fundamentalist to fight the theory of evolution. Evolution sees species developing according to their own potential. But if the species developed through an inner law, there can be no divine significance in the differentiation of the species for the fundamentalist. This may not be too serious in general, and so E. J. Carnell concedes that God may have created original " kinds " that did evolve into the species that we know. But if man evolved from out of other species, then it is difficult to see how he can be uniquely created in the image of God. So Carnell argues that man was one of the original " kinds " created by God, that he did not evolve from other life forms by natural means, that he was especially created by an *ab extra* act.[4]

This view helps to explain the fundamentalist and conservative attitude toward Biblical criticism. Unless the Bible is miraculously beyond natural explanation, it cannot be the Word of God. To reveal the God who is separate from this world, the Bible must be, as Carnell puts it, " an *ab extra* entrance into history of propositions inaccessible to experience." [5] The inerrancy of the Bible is the miraculous mark of its divine origin. If the Bible is analyzable by methods used on other ancient books, as the higher critic supposes, if it was produced by normal human means, subject to the errors to which all humanity is prone, then it could not be the miraculous Word of God.

The liberal believed that fundamentalism discredited the Christian faith. The denial of natural methods of explaining the "miraculous" events put the fundamentalist into open conflict with science. The attempt to suppress the teaching of evolution was symbolic, to the liberal, of the obscurantism into which fundamentalism led. And, worse still, in each battle the scientist was winning. Christianity seemed to require intellectual hara-kiri.

The fundamentalist insisted that the miracles were necessary as proof of the revelation and of Jesus' divinity. But the liberal found himself trying to preach Christianity to a world in which, far from proving Christianity, the miracles were a chief reason why men abandoned it. Liberals who accepted the divinity of Jesus were often prepared to admit that he could be expected to perform miracles. But, they pointed out, such acts no longer have apologetic value. On the contrary, in the modern world a man only comes to believe in the miracles after he has been persuaded of Jesus' divinity on other grounds. Instead of the miracles winning acceptance for the divinity of Jesus, it was belief in the divinity of Jesus that won acceptance for the miracles.

Finally, liberals found that the fundamentalist view of transcendence led to a dangerous apologetic. Inasmuch as evidence for God was found in miraculous acts of intervention, it became a common defensive strategy of Christians to point to gaps in scientific knowledge and to argue that at this point there must be the miraculous intervention of God. But science is continually filling in these gaps, and thus men get the impression that science is destroying, step by step, all reasons for believing in God.

This is a point that we need to take seriously. Many Christians still cling to the argument, "No scientist has explained where life came from; nor has he produced life in his test tube." That is, while science has removed gap after gap where once God's intervention was believed to be the answer, the all-important fact of life stands solidly as a witness to the great gap in our knowledge that only God can fill. But this is a precarious refuge, for the scientists are coming closer to giving a natural explanation of the origin of life and to producing life in their test tubes. When that day occurs, many a minister is going to be faced with disturbing questions.

Liberalism met all these problems with its doctrine of the immanence of God. The liberal doctrine of immanence came from many sources, and varied from liberal to liberal. But William Newton Clarke presents a typical liberal view, and we can illustrate the central point from his thought.

The liberal did not begin with the picture of God and the world as essentially separated. Instead, he saw God acting in the world in a natural and nonmiraculous manner. Whereas fundamentalism feared that the divine significance was taken from an event when it was shown to have natural causes, the liberal saw God working within and through natural causation. As Clarke put it:

> "If law is uniformity of method in the universe, then law, instead of justifying the inference that no mind is present, indicates the presence of a mind so far-seeing as to know that uniformity is good for the universe, so wise as to establish a method in which uniformity will be beneficent, and so powerful and calm as to exercise uniformity in action with unvarying steadiness." [6]

In other words, a naturalistic and a theological explanation of the same event are quite possible and not in conflict with each other. The scientist can find how life evolved slowly through the centuries, and the theologian can see the hand of God moving through the laws discovered by the scientist. A conflict between science and theology is ruled out in principle. No scientific finding can damage theology because it does not give a theological explanation; no theology can contradict science because theology is not a scientific explanation. There can be conflict only when, forgetting their business, scientists become amateur theologians or theologians become amateur scientists.

If this concept of immanence were taken to an extreme, it would result in pantheism, the identification of God with the universe. Humanists and some other left-wing liberals accepted this, but the center of liberalism was always careful to avoid it. As Clarke put it:

"By the immanence of God is meant that he is everywhere and always present in the universe, nowhere absent from it, never separated from its life. By his transcendence is meant, not (as is sometimes represented) that he is outside and views the universe from beyond and above, but that he is not shut up in it, not limited by it, not required in his totality to maintain and order it. By both together is meant that he is a free Spirit, inhabiting the universe but surpassing it — immanent, as always in the universe, and transcendent, as always independent of its limitations and able to act upon it." [7]

When we see these differing pictures of the relation of God and the universe, we can understand much of the conflict between liberalism and fundamentalism. The Biblical picture of creation was extolled by the fundamentalist because the supernatural God is pictured as creating the world apart from himself, fashioning man apart from the rest of nature and breathing life into him. On the other hand, evolution was most congenial to the liberal. Here he could see God patiently working through the order of his own creation, finally bringing man from out of the lower levels of life by a natural process. This debate was far more than a question of whether Genesis is to be taken literally. It was a life-and-death struggle between two radically opposed philosophies of God's activity in the world.

A miraculously inerrant Bible went naturally with the fundamentalist picture, as we have seen. But the liberal found it more congenial to his view of God that God revealed himself in the Bible by working through natural means. Again we may quote Clarke:

"It is often thought that a historical revelation of God must require more than ordinary historical evidence to prove it; that what is supernatural must needs be supernaturally attested. But this assumption is neither correct nor helpful to Christianity. If a special divine presence in certain events of history cannot be learned from the facts when they are fairly known by ordinary means, it cannot be established at all." [8]

"Neo-orthodoxy" is often defined in terms of its revolt against the immanence of the liberals. It brought many charges against their views, but the most important are probably the following:

First, it was argued that the liberals had lost sight of the distance between God and man. Man at his best was seen as continuous with God. With the idea of God working within the world, the liberals tended to find God within the self. Because God was seen as working in and through history, liberals came to identify the Kingdom of God with a historical system that man, with God's help, could build on earth. The immanent God was so close to nature that liberalism came to believe that God could be discovered as the laws of nature are discovered through patient research. Thus the uniqueness of the Biblical religion, with God's search for man, was lost, and the Bible was seen as an interesting page in the ongoing search of man for God. And in this process the personal nature of God was blurred; God became the rational order of the universe, or was identified with the Absolute of idealist philosophy or with the Principle of Concretion in Whitehead.

The neo-orthodox movement never has denied that God works immanently in the world. But it has been concerned to emphasize that God is not the world, nor the best in man. God is " totally other," in essence separated from the world. Thus God is not to be known by examining the best in man or the world. Man's goodness and knowledge are always under God's judgment. Consequently, although God is known in revelation, he is also always and everywhere the hidden God; he transcends all that we know about him. Our knowledge of God must always confess humbly that it fades away into mystery before the Sovereign Lord of all. And neo-orthodoxy has been concerned to affirm God's freedom to act within the world as he wills to do. In short, neo-orthodoxy has been concerned to attack the tendency to make man's life, religion, moral experience, etc., the center of theology. In place of this it has asserted the absolute centrality of God for Christian faith.

This brief summary of the current situation in theology makes it clear that it is not enough to argue the debate simply in terms of transcendence or immanence, since these terms do not possess sufficiently sharp meanings. We shall try to state a position for a new reformation theology that will deal with immanence and transcendence in terms of causality, epistemology, morality, history, eschatology, and personality.

An important aspect of the debate is concerned with the relation of God's causal action within the world. Causally, it seems to me that liberalism's immanence was essentially sound and more orthodox than conservatism. The conservative, Carl Henry, charges liberalism with inventing a dualism within truth by dividing scientific truth from theological truth.[9] This charge seems to be based upon the assumption that " causality " should have only one dimension of meaning, and that if a natural cause for an event is found, it cannot also have a supernatural cause. Hence, if evolution demonstrates that natural causes produced man, we can no longer believe that man is created in the image of God.

But even within our natural universe we know that an event may be causally described in more than one way without one description canceling out the other. For example, I raise my hand and ask what is the cause of this. Physiologically this event can be explained fully in terms of muscular expansion and contraction in response to electrical actions originating in the brain and transmitted through the nerve cells. This explanation can be made complete and it satisfactorily explains the raised hand on one level of interpretation. But it is also possible to explain this event fully and completely by saying that it was caused by my desire to illustrate a theoretical point. The fact that the physiological explanation can be made does not nullify the validity of the mental explanation; nor does the mental nullify the physiological. Which of the two explanations will be satisfactory will depend upon the particular purpose the questioner had in mind when he asked why the hand was raised.

John Macmurray finds this distinction so important that he suggests that we should not apply the term " cause " to the functioning of the mind. It is a radically different means of explanation.[10] And Brunner, in the same vein, asserts that " causality " should not be applied to God's relationship to the world since cause is a term that takes its meaning from the relationship between created objects and hence cannot be applied properly to the Creator's activity.[11] Regardless of what we call these different explanations, it is obvious that two radically different explanations of a single event are quite possible and normal.

I am not trying to say that the action of the mind is a perfect analogy of God's activity. God is not the "mind" of the physical universe. But this is to point out that there is nothing strange about two explanations of the same event on different levels. The liberal's view of God's causal immanence is no more a dividing of truth than are the two explanations of why a hand is raised. The liberal simply affirms that a theological and a scientific explanation of the same event are compatible with each other since they explain on different levels. It is because such various explanations are possible that Niebuhr argues that the Biblical " myths " are not simply prescientific, but are also suprascientific interpretations. Thus the Genesis story of creation is in no sense in competition with scientific views of the origin of the universe. It explains the universe on a different level from that of science.

The fundamentalist position was discredited every time that it entered into conflict with science. And it is obvious why it was. God is not a scientific hypothesis, and God's " causal " activity is not a natural event. The astronomer Laplace is often quoted for his famous statement about God: " I have no need of that hypothesis." This is quite true — the scientist who uses God to fill a gap in his scientific knowledge is resorting to a *deus ex machina* to hide his ignorance. God's created world has an independent existence, and its operation can be studied and explained fully upon the natural level by science. Theology, therefore, should never fear the findings of science, for science cannot, in the nature of the case, refute a theological understanding of an event. This applies to the science of Biblical criticism as well as to any other science.

If we look for God's activity where there is no natural, scientific explanation of the event, we doom ourselves to an everlasting battle with science. The realm of nature will continue to grow, and the realm of God's activity will shrink. This is true not only with events like the origin of life, behind which we can still hide, but it is true even in the case of the Biblical miracles. If a miracle marks the supernatural intervention of God into his universe and is necessary to prove that God is at work, we face the problem that, until the scientific venture is complete, we cannot know what is a miracle.

Thus, when psychotherapy developed to the point where it accepted many of the healing miracles of Jesus, it was not a victory but a loss for fundamentalism. We could now believe that the healings had occurred, but they were no longer miraculous in the sense of being a suspension of natural law.

We do not have space here to develop a doctrine of miracle. Such a doctrine is vital to Christianity, for miracle is a fundamental and indispensable part of its faith. But for the present purposes, we must insist that it is useless to define miracle as a direct causal intervention of God into the natural order. Until we have a complete knowledge of nature, we cannot know what is miraculous. As the healing miracles have been made to seem natural by the development of psychotherapy, miracles like walking on water may be made to seem natural by the development of paranormal psychology and psychic research.

It must be emphasized that, believing as we do that God is the Creator of the world, we do not deny that God can act again in his world with his creative power and perform miracles in this sense. In fact, it is quite reasonable to suppose that he can and does. But our point is that this cannot be made the defining mark of what a miracle is, for then we could not know when a miracle had occurred. Miracles are not a question of science or for science; they are a question of the theological interpretation of events. Faith, not science, beholds the miraculous, because a miracle is any event in which the eyes of faith see God making himself manifest.

The naturalist, like the conservative, denies that there can be two explanations of the same event — a scientific and a theological one. The naturalist denies it, however, from the point of view of naturalism, which says that there is nothing to which we can refer beyond nature. The naturalist sees the world as the extreme behaviorist sees human activity. The behaviorist sees no significance in the purpose for which I raised my hand; the naturalist sees no purpose behind nature. But these are positions that can only be believed; they cannot be verified. Science does nothing to confirm them. They are *fides* decisions about what facts are significant. If supernaturalism means that there are nonnatural causes that operate by suspending natural law, science can disprove this by showing the natural causes for every event thought to be supernatural. But if supernaturalism does not deny the natural explanation but insists that the same events are explainable in a different dimension, science cannot speak for or against the claim. Science can show that an event has a natural system of causes, as it can show the function of the brain and the nervous system in bodily movement. But science cannot in the nature of the case prove that there is not a nonscientific explanation of the same event, just as science cannot prove that purpose, will, and reason were not real factors in the bodily movement.

We have made the claim that liberalism at this point is more orthodox than conservatism. To prove this decisively would take several chapters of historical research. But we can mention the following: The Bible itself is in harmony in many places with this view of God. The Bible makes it clear that the performance of a miracle in no way proves the truth of what the miracle worker says. (Deut. 13:1-3; Matt. 24:24.) Although modern man is often annoyed at the amount of miracle in the Bible, nonetheless, among the religious records of mankind, the Bible is very sober about relating miracle stories.

Many Biblical events in which God's action is seen are also events explainable, as the Bible recognizes, on natural grounds. One of the most crucial events in the Old Testament is the taking of the Jews into and out of the Babylonian exile. The prophets make it clear that these are revealing and redemptive acts of God. But they are also events that occur in history by normal historical means. The fact that human armies and power politics are involved as causal factors in these events does not lead the prophets to deny their divine basis. In the New Testament, to use only one illustration, Christ's death is the mightiest of God's mighty acts, and yet the New Testament makes it clear that Judas, Caiaphas, Pilate, and the crowd acted causally in the event in a purely natural way. At the very least we can affirm that our interpretation of God's " causal " activity is not contrary to the Bible.

In the history of Christian thought, this view of God's activity

has played a definite role. Augustine explicitly rejected the view
that God operates on the universe from the outside. God, he tells us,
did not create the world as a carpenter makes a chest, for the carpenter is external to that which he makes and he operates on it
from outside himself. But God is everywhere present in his creation
and governs it by his continual presence within it.[12] As a result,
Augustine saw clearly that a natural cause of an event did not mean
that God was not the ultimate cause of the event. He even went so
far as to speculate that the living things of the world had been
created in the form of hidden seeds, or " seminal causes," and God's
providence caused these to develop into the life forms as we know
them, a theory that has been interpreted as an early doctrine of evolution.[13] This may be going too far, but it is certainly safe to say
that Augustine would not have feared to accept the modern theory
of evolution.

Augustine does not even draw an absolute line between God's
natural means of working and miracles. The mark of a miracle for
Augustine is not its suspension of the normal means of God's
activity, but its unusual nature. A miracle is not primarily an un-
natural event; on the contrary, it is quite natural, but it occurs
unexpectedly and in an unusual time and manner. And as such it
calls man's attention to the presence of God's activity.[14] This theory
seems in essential agreement with the Bible where a miracle is made
miraculous because it is an event in which God's activity and will is
made manifest or brought to the attention of the beholders. Whether
or not natural laws have been suspended or broken is immaterial
to its miraculous nature. I believe that it is safe to say that if the
Augustinian insights had been maintained, there would have been
no science-religion controversy.

In the Middle Ages the concept of a dualistic supernaturalism
was growing, but the great philosophers always maintained God's
causal immanence. For example, it has become conventional to interpret the cosmological proof of God as saying that each effect
has a cause, and that cause has a cause, and so on until finally we
have to assume the first cause in the series. So interpreted, of course,
the cosmological argument is easily disposed of. Who, then, caused

the first cause? Why cannot the series be infinite? But anyone who is prepared to spend half an hour in examining Aquinas will realize that this is not what he was saying at all. Aquinas never supposed that the First Cause was the temporal first in the series, a super-natural cause that started the chain of natural causes. On the contrary, God as the First Cause is a cause upon a completely different level from natural causation. As Maritain has put it:

"It is clear that not only the being, but also the action of all other causes, or the causality itself which they exercise, depend at every moment on that first cause. . . . If then we consider the relation of any efficient cause whatever to the First Cause, we see that this efficient cause would not act at any moment at all if, at that very moment, it were not activated by the First Cause." [15]

It is quite clear that Aquinas would have no reason to see God's activity denied because a natural cause for an event like the formation of life or of man was found. The natural cause so found could only be a cause at all because of the continuing operation of God, the First Cause.

Calvin repudiates the idea that God was creator only for a moment at the beginning of the universe. God is continually and creatively at work in the world. Without in any way denying the natural causation of all events, Calvin asserts that " not a drop of rain falls but at the express command of God." Furthermore, Calvin's view of God's governance of the world was so complete that he did not distinguish sharply between the action of God in miracles and God's normal action. He says:

"When he would have Jonah thrown into the sea, he sent forth a wind to raise a tempest. It will be said by them who suppose God not to hold the helm of the world, that this was a deviation from the common course of things. But the conclusion which I deduce from it is, that no wind ever rises or blows but by the special command of God." [16]

It is impossible to understand Calvin's doctrine of predestination if we think of God's predestining causal action operating instead of man's natural will. God's causality acts through man's will and not instead of it. "Man falls, therefore, according to the appointment of Divine Providence; but he falls by his own fault." [17] In many ways Calvin carries the causal immanence of God's activity farther than we are prepared to do, but he certainly cannot be quoted in favor of a dualistically transcendent form of causality.

In a scientific age the most reasonable interpretation of God's "causality" is in terms of its action within a dimension other than that of the causality of natural causes. The one does not negate the other. Belief in the reality of God's causality, which is seen by faith, in no way discourages or denies the legitimacy of the scientific search for the natural cause of the same event. When the scientist produces life in his test tube it will not prove that God's hand was not the ultimate cause of life's creation. Not only is this interpretation fitting in a scientific age; it is in harmony with the best in Christian theology and with the Bible itself.

Turning from causal to epistemological considerations, we find the area in which the new reformation movement has been most concerned to stress transcendence. In the light of the space we have spent on revelation and the question of reason and faith, it is not necessary to expand this point. God is epistemologically transcendent in the sense that God cannot be known simply from the study of the universe or man. Certainly the believer sees God's hand in nature, but he sees it because he looks at nature from the perspective given by revelation. God is known only where God wills to be known; in revelation God is free to reveal himself where he wills. And even in revelation God is hidden as well as revealed. God does not force himself upon our attention; he does not over-power us with unanswerable arguments. God speaks hiddenly in Christ, and his hidden word demands a decision of faith from the hearer. Consequently, our language about God must be symbolic language; God is never simply describable in terms of our usual language. In revelation we truly know God, but our knowledge never exhausts God's reality. His ways are not our ways.

Another aspect of God's transcendence is moral transcendence. This is expressed by the concept of the holiness of God. In the presence of God man knows that his moral best is not good enough.

There is no place for boasting before God; when we have done all things, we must count ourselves as unprofitable servants. This is also joined with epistemological considerations in that we are unable to know God by means of examining man's moral life. Our best morality remains under the judgment of God. Furthermore, the Christian revelation reveals that man is a sinner. This is the sharpest of all divisions between man and God and the division that makes it impossible to identify God with man's moral history and life.

Despite the holy transcendence of God over our moral attainments, from the perspective of the Christian faith, we can see that as God works through natural causation, so he has worked through man's moral life. Moral knowledge does not of itself lead to God, but when the gospel comes it speaks to the man who knows right from wrong. The Christian, looking back, can see that God was working through the moral life to prepare him for Christ. (Gal. 3:24.)

A most important aspect of the transcendence of the Biblical God is his historical freedom. That is, unlike the God of mystic philosophers, like the God of Erigena, God is under no necessity to create. Creation is never the natural emanation of the world from its source in God; instead, God decides to create. In the same way, God's action in history is never a necessity; God is not bound by his creation. When man sins, we have no a priori way of knowing what God's reaction will be. We believe that God will forgive repentant sinners, not because we know that God must forgive them or even that they "ought" to be forgiven. We know it only because the cross of Christ promises that they will be forgiven.

The Biblical God takes time seriously, and thus we have a history of God's redemption in the Bible. Redemption is not a timeless process, flowing by necessity from God, but it is dependent upon the free decisions made by God and upon his acts of redemption which are immanent within historical time. Because God takes time seriously, we can speak of his transcendence in terms of historical freedom. Because he chooses to act in history, we can speak of his immanence within history.

Rationalists always have shrunk from this view of God. They have seen God as timeless, as eternally ruled by his rational laws, so that God's behavior is, in principle, predictable. But the Bible never presents God this way. Sometimes in a most naïve way it proclaims God's historical transcendence or freedom by picturing God as deliberating what he shall do or even as repenting of his past acts. (Gen. 6:6.)

This means that man never has any hold or claim upon God. God is not to be manipulated or controlled by those who know his secrets. This was the great insight of Luther. As a monastic Catholic, Luther sought to fulfill the known prerequisites so that he could stand before God demanding his salvation. But Luther came to see that this was blasphemy; it is to put God at man's disposal. We have no way of manipulating God; we are dependent solely upon the good will of God's free decision. And hence we cannot know that we must be saved; we can only trust the promise made to us by the gracious God. Christian faith thus becomes the radical decision that the God revealed in Christ can be trusted.

Another aspect of the transcendence of the Biblical God is personal transcendence. The person of God and the person of man must be sharply distinguished. Mysticism, even within Christianity, has tended always to see God and man merged. Thus the Christian mystic Eckhart could say, "The eye with which I see God is the same as that with which he sees me." In the mystic experience God and man are blended into one, and the distinction between them disappears. In popular thought this is often expressed by saying that there is a " little bit of God in every man." God is thus found within man and his consciousness. Liberalism, with its emphasis upon the immanence of God and religious experience, was never completely free from the danger of falling into such mysticism. Rufus Jones, who expressed liberalism in some of its finest aspects and who never lost his grounding in the Christian faith, could nonetheless make remarks like this: " There is one door that opens into a holy of holies. The true path is through personality. The search must *begin* in our own bosom." [18] Where the door to knowing God is made our own bosoms, we are in continual danger of identifying God with our "higher" selves. Jones was only partly saved from this by his strong emphasis upon the revelation of God in Christ.

The truth in all mysticism is the insight that it is not enough to know about God, to observe him from the outside, to quote doctrines about him. God must be known in our deepest experience. But the Biblical God is the God who comes to man, not as the deepest element of himself, but the God who meets man in history and meets him in a truly I-and-thou relationship. God is known in person-to-person conversation. In physics we do not study the psychology of physicists; we study the universe. Similarly, to know God we do not study the religious experience of the believer. In our experience we know God, as the physicist knows the world in his experience; but in each case the object of knowledge is outside and apart from the knower.

The Biblical God is not the oversoul of Emerson, and he is not an element within my self. He is the God who speaks to me and speaks in judgment upon the best within me. Contemporary theology has used words like " encounter " and " confrontation " to describe the Christian experience. Such words have their weakness in that they have a ring of antagonism to them, but they are valuable means of expressing the fact that the Christian is not absorbed into God, that he does not lose himself in religious experience; instead, he finds himself as a self more truly because he is in a person-to-person relationship with God who is other than himself.

Finally, we must preserve what we may call eschatological transcendence. God in his will and purpose is not limited by our space-time existence. Thus it is one of the strengths of neo-orthodoxy that it has insisted that God's Kingdom cannot be an earthly kingdom. The liberal view of immanence often became historical immanence; the Kingdom of God was to be built upon this earth. The age to which liberalism accommodated itself saw history itself as redemptive; it was progressing toward the ideal earthly society. Liberalism at its best was never identified with this viewpoint, but the danger was there and some liberals fell into it as they abandoned all idea of a life after death.

Philip Phenix points out the strange fact that for an overwhelming majority of people the core of religion is its belief in life after death. And yet Protestant theologians devote little attention to the subject and seem disposed to deny personal survival.[19] This has struck me as a peculiar aspect of contemporary thought. It is strange because it is impossible to see how we can speak of the Christian faith at all if it does not include the fact of man's survival of death. Death is one of the foremost enemies that Christ overcame. (I Cor. 15:12-34, 54-57.) If there is no life after death, it seems impossible to maintain belief in the Christian God. If this life is the end for man as an individual, then it is impossible to apply the term "just" to God, much less to say that he is love.

There are many reasons for theology placing a declining emphasis upon personal survival. Heaven often has become a "pie-in-the-sky" promise that appeals to man's selfish instincts and that blinds him to his duties in this life. Emphasis upon the individual's eternal destiny often has fostered an unchristian individualism that ignores society and its claims. But these are perversions of the Christian faith. Christianity takes this historical life as seriously as does the Marxist or the believer in secular progress. Christianity does not promise an escape from history into a timeless eternity, but it does promise the fulfillment of history. History takes on an added importance when it is seen that what occurs in history will have eternal consequences. Furthermore, although each individual must die alone before his God, his life is lived in intimate correlation with his society, and no interpretation of Christianity is adequate that leaves out the social dimension of the Christian hope for fulfillment — the Kingdom of God.

It is strange to find theology soft-pedaling or even dropping the Christian hope of survival beyond death; for the secular world is more aware today than it has been for many centuries that if there is any meaning to our historical existence, it is not a meaning that is immanent within our history. Today total war threatens to destroy history in a sudden and violent end. Even if the whole past of history can be reversed and an ideal earthly society built, those who have lived through the thousands of past years have bloomed unseen and wasted their sweetness on the desert air of an unfulfilled existence, for they will not participate in the final ideal society.

This is one form of transcendence that is crucial to the Christian faith. It is a form of transcendence that our world is prepared again to consider as relevant. It recognizes that God's will, person, and purpose include more than this earthly creation. Because God transcends his creation, his purpose for man is never exhausted by this life or this history. Christianity does not offer man a simple " existential " fulfillment here and now; it does not offer him simply a meaning for this life. It places before him a challenge that he is often afraid to grasp — he has been called for eternity itself.

The Biblical faith presents us with a God who is transcendent over his creation and yet who is immanently active and at work within it. As a result there will always be a tension in Christian thought at this point. From the perspective of a new reformation faith it is not enough to argue about immanence and transcendence in general. There are many levels upon which the two concepts are relevant and which we must consider. I have tried to point out several of these. Because the Christian affirms both transcendence and immanence for God, he will not claim that one or the other of these concepts applies simply and in the same way to all areas in which the terms are applicable. This is an area of theology that still needs a much more complete analysis.

VI.

Sin

Sɪɴ is a most unpopular word that has become intellectually re-spectable again in our time. We have emerged only recently from a period that found no use for the concept of sin. The scientific theory of evolution was made the cornerstone of a doctrine of on-going progress toward the ideal society. The barriers to be over-come did not include sin; they consisted of the inertia of the past, ignorance, and maladjustment. Science, spread by education and controlled democratically, was destined to save mankind. Even Christian proclamations ceased emphasizing sin.

But a change has occurred, a change so dramatic that it is still difficult to comprehend its nature. Many factors led to this change in climate. The findings of depth psychology disturbed man's faith in sweet reasonableness. Beneath man's rational exterior it was re-vealed that there lurk hidden rationalizations, grim urges, and dark secrets. But more important were the historical events of our age. A world that fought and won the war to end all wars and to make the world safe for democracy encountered new totalitarianisms that brought back the horrors of the dark ages. The science that was to save and free man has produced brainwashing, sputniks, and war on a more horrible scale. The extermination of six million Jews in one of the most civilized and scientifically advanced na-tions burned an impression upon our conscience. We are living in a century when it seems that man is capable of doing anything he wishes to do except to live in peace, justice, and harmony with his fellow men.

The doctrine of sin has played a large role in contemporary theo-logical discussion. Neo-orthodoxy first arose in America by criticiz-

ing the " shallow view of sin " in liberalism. But before neo-orthodoxy arrived on the scene the conservatives were making the same
criticism. Thus J. G. Machen charged that liberals could deny
miracles and supernatural salvation because they had ignored the
depths of man's sin.[1]

There is truth in these charges against liberalism. In their attempt to meet the modern world, the liberals tended to minimize
the Christian doctrine of sin in an age that had little willingness to
listen to such teaching. We could collect many quotations from liberals to show this. Thus Lyman Abbott could say, " The individual
man is partly the animal from which he has come, and partly the
God who is coming into him; but God is steadily displacing the
animal." [2] But at no point is a sweeping criticism of liberalism more
unfair. The sober center of liberal thought was never unaware of
the reality of sin, and its " pessimism " at this point was in marked
contrast to the optimism of the age.

Liberals did repudiate any doctrine of inherited sin. Not only did
they deny the Genesis story of Adam and Eve, but they also insisted
that the very idea of an inherited sin was a contradiction in terms.
No man can be held responsible for another's sin. But from this it
did not follow that the liberal took a shallow view of man's sin.
W. N. Clarke pointed out that " the fact [of sin] is ' writ large '
upon the face of the Christian revelation, that man to whom it is
addressed is a sinful being, individually and as a race. Never is he
otherwise represented save as God has changed him." [3] Clarke asserts
that this Biblical witness is verified by the common moral judgment
of mankind. He even uses the Genesis story of the Fall, in which
he finds the truth that sin disrupts the destiny for which man was
created and thus is in a real sense a " fall " of man. " In consequence
of this perverted strain in the transmitted humanity, children are
not born either wholly good or neutral between good and evil, but
with evil tendencies which grow into sin when responsible life
begins." [4]

In spite of the liberals' understanding of sin, the conservatives
and the neo-orthodox remained dissatisfied with liberalism. They
found, even in liberals who recognized the problem of sin, a

tendency to see the possibility of its cure within man himself. Thus Clarke, despite his sober estimate of man's sinful nature, could say, "Humanity certainly is by nature a slowly rising race, with a native tendency to outgrow faults." [5] Barth and others charged that liberalism was not calling man to the repentant state where he would throw himself upon God; liberalism was still appealing to man himself to overcome the problem of sin.

Conservatism went farther and insisted that liberalism could never see the seriousness of sin while it refused to accept the historical nature of Genesis. Man, the conservative asserted, is guilty and tainted with the weakness of sin because of Adam's sin. Adam was the federal representative for man; Adam's actions were our actions; "Adam's sin and its dread results have therefore been imputed to his descendants, put to their account, charged legally to them. . . . All men today have mortal bodies, corrupted souls, inborn tendencies to sin, and the sentence of everlasting death upon them apart from Christ." [6] As the conservative sees it, therefore, even the neo-orthodox theologian who dwells on sin cannot really see its serious nature since he denies the historicity of Adam and Eve.

The new reformation concern with sin is so well known, and has been developed so fully in several studies, that I feel no need to develop it here. [7] Instead, I shall try to make a few comments upon the present scene in theology and point out a few personal conclusions.

Behind the rediscovery of orthodoxy in our times there lies above all else the rediscovery of the reality of sin. The various branches of the new reformation theology have no unanimous agreement upon questions of reason and faith, eschatology, and many others. But they are united in agreement that there is a realism in orthodox Christianity's view of human nature that we must reaffirm.

It is often charged that this is nothing but a pessimistic reaction to the sorry events of the twentieth century, a failure of nerve in light of two world wars, the rise of totalitarianism, the great depression, the Korean "incident," the slaughter of six million Jews, the cold war, the threat of atomic destruction, and racial discrimination. If this is the case, we may assume that when the world "gets

back to normal " these prophets of doom and gloom will go the way
of all outdated thinkers.

To this, however, we might say several things. Even if this is a
" failure of nerve," it is hardly surprising, for the list of catastrophes
in our century is truly impressive. They cannot be brushed aside by
any facile talk about keeping up our chins, thinking positively, and
remembering that man's time on earth has been short compared to
the geological ages. Any man who could live through this century
and not feel his nerve failing would be in a serious psychological
state of divorcement from reality. American Christians sometimes
sneer at the "pessimism" of their European brethren and blame
the decadence of a " dying European culture." But as we look at
the world, we must ask whether it is not our optimism that is the
aberration. Is this optimism anything more than the reflection of
the relative security that, until recently, America has enjoyed? The
rush of frantic terror in America that met the news of Russia's
space-satellites would indicate that we have been living in a dream
world.

We might also ask what it means to return to " normal times."
In taking a long view of history, are not our days more normal than
the idyllic years that the upper-middle-class Europeans and Americans knew during the later nineteenth and the early twentieth centuries? In short, the weight of history would make it appear that
the new orthodoxy has analyzed history faithfully and that liberal
optimism is the reflection of a period that is now past.

We must be careful, however, in arguing too easily from the
woes of the world to the Christian doctrine of sin. In no sense do
the problems of our times prove the doctrine of sin. For the Christian doctrine of sin is not a sociological or a psychological analysis
of man's life; it is teaching about man's relationship to God. That
man has got himself into a mess is something that anyone can verify
by reading the daily paper, but that man got into the mess because
he is a sinner is something that man knows only when he sees life
from the perspective of the Christian faith. In other words, the
Christian doctrine of sin should not become more likely in an age of
war and rumor of war and less likely in an age of prosperity and

peace. Of course, faith here too seeks understanding; and although the faith in inevitable progress finds it difficult to understand the events of our century, the Christian is able to see that Christianity has always told us that there would be days like this. The events of our century are certainly understandable within the Christian perspective, but they cannot be said to prove it.

Recent theology has been deeply interested in modern literature and art in which it feels that it finds a more profound analysis of man than it finds in much religious writing. Our writers and artists have revealed the seething depths of the human consciousness and man's estrangement, anxiety, and sense of guilt. We are often told that movies like *Baby Doll* have deeper theological implications than the ostensibly religious movies like *The Ten Commandments*. This is a healthy concern in theology; the artists can often see the depths of the age in which they live more clearly than the social scientist, the clergyman, or the man on the street. But it is quite wrong to suppose that we can find the Christian doctrine of sin in Albert Camus, Tennessee Williams, or Jean-Paul Sartre. What we can find in such men is material that the Christian doctrine of sin can illuminate. On the other hand, Christian novelists, like Graham Greene or C. S. Lewis, can portray vividly for us the Christian doctrine of sin, but they do it precisely because their novels have a dimension lacking in most contemporary novels.

The reason that an analysis of current events or a study of contemporary literature cannot show us the Christian doctrine of sin is that the doctrine implies the whole background of the Christian faith. It is not one item that can be proved by itself; it forms a part of the whole and will stand or fall with the whole. It is not unusual today to find secularist intellectuals who accept Reinhold Niebuhr's analysis of sin but reject the rest of his theology. But what such men miss is that in rejecting the rest of Niebuhr's theology, they no longer have Niebuhr's doctrine of man, but have simply a pessimistic and even cynical view of human nature.

In the language of the Reformation we can say that what current events show us are the *sins* of man. But no analysis of current events can demonstrate the *sin* of man. Current events show man commit-

ting sins, but faith alone knows that he commits them because he is
a sinner.

What, then, is the Christian doctrine of sin? The Christian believes that man was created in the image of God; he was given dignity and the right to have dominion over all the creatures of the
earth. Christ, as the " Second Adam," reveals to us what man was
meant to be, so that in Jesus' life of fellowship with and dependence
upon God we find the life that man was created to live.

Man sins because his high place in creation tempts him to forget
that he is a creature, and so he longs to be equal to the Creator. Instead of allowing God to be the center of his life, man attempts to
put himself at the center. When man is at the center of his own life,
he can no longer love his neighbor as God would have him love.
Man's sin is thus his separation from God, resulting from his refusal to let God be the center of his life. From this sin comes man's
sins, his evil deeds against his fellow men. Sin means that man lives
unnaturally; he does not live as he was created to live; he has fallen.
Thus man becomes anxious; he feels lost and alone in the universe;
he becomes the kind of creature that we see staring at us from the
pages of so many modern novels.

But, the conservative says, how can you believe this if you do not
accept the historicity of Adam and Eve? First, we must affirm that
in dealing with man's sin we are entering the final limits of thought.
Here reason fails because we are trying to comprehend the ultimate
irrationality. The Garden of Eden story is a profound parable that
illuminates the relationship of God and man. The truth of the story
is no more dependent upon a historical Adam and Eve than the
truth of the parable of the prodigal son depends upon the events'
having actually occurred before Jesus told the parable. In the Genesis
story we see portrayed in a vivid and poetic way the fact that man
was created in God's image. But man longs to be God and so falls
to the serpent's trick. (Gen. 3:5.) From this refusal to accept God
as God, man loses his original innocence and free fellowship with
God. He is cast from the Garden.

The truth of the Genesis story does not stand or fall with the
question of whether it would be possible to locate the Garden of

Eden geographically. We accept the story because it "speaks to our condition." Here we find the light that illuminates our lives; here is the analysis of sin that makes sense out of the nonsense of life. Man falls into sin when, refusing to accept his place of high dignity under God, he grasps for equality with God. This is the problem that is set right only when Christ, the Second Adam, does not grasp for equality with God, even though he has the right to do so (Phil. 2:5-8), but humbles himself and gives "his life a ransom for many" (Matt. 20:28). The Christian affirms the truth in the Adam and Eve story, regardless of its historicity, because it is in complete correlation with the redemption the Christian has found in Christ.

The term "original sin" inevitably grates upon the sensitivities of modern man. But the term, despite its misuses, must be retained. It points up the fact that all man's sins stem from his original sin, the sin that is logically first. Man sins because he is a sinner in the wrong relationship with God; he sins because he has tried to place himself, his concerns, his insights, at the center of his life, where God ought to be. It is also original in the sense that it describes a situation that we inherit. Theoretically it seems that every man should begin again from scratch, with a completely free choice between a life of good or evil. A priori thinking always begins with this presupposition. But an a posteriori look at life as it is lived will not allow us to hold this. Sin is something that has somehow got its hold upon the human race as a whole. No man ever got into the Kingdom of God by following the line of least resistance; nor did he even find an equal resistance to the Kingdom of God and the kingdom of evil. No man can claim that when he is "doing what comes naturally" he loves his neighbor as himself. Whatever one thinks of the doctrine that Adam was our federal representative who took us into sin with him, that doctrine does point up the fact that humanity is somehow a whole, that we cannot vote ourselves out of the human race. When we follow the Reformation and pray, "Lord, we are by nature sinful and unclean," it is not pious nonsense, but a sober analysis of man as we find him. Certainly if we believe that Christ was the Second Adam, man as God intends man to be, we can only confess that something is radically wrong with the whole human race. Even if there were no story of Adam and Eve, the Christian doctrine of Christ would lead us to a doctrine of original sin.

One of the difficulties about taking the story of Adam and Eve literally is that it has harnessed the Christian faith with the un-christian doctrine of an inherited guilt. In our quotation above from a conservative source, we find the teaching that today man is held "legally" responsible for the sin committed by Adam. This doctrine has always outraged the moral conscience of man, and rightly so. It is absurd to punish one man for the crime committed by another. But for the Christian the problem is that such a con-cept cannot be reconciled with the revelation of God in Christ.

Christ called men to repent for their own sins, not for the sins of other men, much less of Adam. There are still those who try to justify their anti-Semitism with the argument that the Jews cruci-fied Christ and are therefore damned. We should never try to meet this by proving that the Romans, not the Jews, crucified Christ. For then it seems that we should be anti-Italian, instead of anti-Semitic. The Christian answer to this is that no matter who crucified Jesus, no man today can be guilty of what was done by his ancestors two thousand years ago. In the same way, we cannot reconcile the impu-tation of Adam's guilt to his descendants. We do not need any help from Adam to make us guilty; our own sin is quite sufficient for that.

The idea of an inherited sin in Christian thought is the result of a confusion of terms. Biblical sin and guilt are personal, not legal terms. Legally you might impute one man's crime to another man, even if it were unjust to do so. But sin is a matter of personal rela-tionships. Sin begins with a man's loss of the Father-son relation-ship with God; it consists of setting himself at the center of life where God ought to be; it is a denial of God's claim upon him. To say that a man is a sinner and that he is guilty before God is to say something about *his* relationship to God; it says nothing about his forefathers. It is significant that even Calvin, with his doctrine of predestination, was concerned to show that each man is responsible for his own guilt and his own rejection by God. Thus he says that sinful men "intentionally suppress the cause of condemnation, which they are constrained to acknowledge in themselves, hoping to excuse themselves by charging it upon God." [8]

Man, as we find him in the light of Christ, is a sinner. He is "curved in upon himself." Instead of obeying God, he tries to live by his own light. This is the original sin of man which has been known as "pride." The term "pride" often leads to misunderstanding. For example, the term "pride" in Reinhold Niebuhr's analysis of sin has led to much criticism based upon a misunderstanding of his position. Ministers and psychiatrists object that they seldom meet people with an inflated or prideful ego, but they continually meet people with feelings of inferiority or guilt complexes. But such criticisms are based on a misreading of Niebuhr. Thus Niebuhr can say, "From the Christian standpoint the self-hatred which is supposed to make love impossible is actually the consequence of a too anxious preoccupation with self." [9] Pride has come to mean a "swelled head" in our language. But pride, in Christian theology, as Niebuhr uses it, means an overconcern with the self. The man who is curved in on himself and preoccupied with himself is a man who will be deeply disturbed if he finds any inadequacies in himself, and thus he is a man who may be suffering from an "inferiority complex" or from guilt feelings. "Self-centeredness," although it too has disadvantages, seems a better term to describe the Christian doctrine of sin. But it must be understood over against the view that man is created to be God-centered.

Because man is, by nature, curved in upon himself, men tend to judge events in terms of the effects upon themselves. Niebuhr summarizes it, "All men are persistently inclined to regard themselves more highly and are more assiduously concerned with their own interests than any 'objective' view of their importance would warrant." [10] Thus men tend to form political judgments that closely parallel their own personal interests. America, as a nation, was stirred to aid the suffering of humanity after World War II only when, to humanitarian appeals, was linked the appeal of self-interest. The aid was given to stop communism. The academic thinker may overlook this point, but the canny politician is aware that the

appeal to men's self-interest must never be too far from the surface
if he is to get results.

Because man is curved in on himself, all his acts of righteousness
are tainted with self-righteousness. Man always tends to see his
deeds as more righteous than they are. He can see the chicanery
in every generous act of his enemy, but blithely expects his own
overtures of good will to be taken at their face value. He identifies
his own good with a higher good and thus seeks self-gain even in
his " altruism." America is disturbed that the countries into which
it has poured economic aid are not more grateful for this benefi-
cence. The charitable rich have always found this lack in the poor.
But the reason is not far to find. Every act of generosity is tainted
with some feeling of superiority and self-righteousness on the part of
the giver. The receiver senses this, and because it threatens his own
self-esteem he resents it and refuses to grovel in his gratitude.

Reinhold Niebuhr, building on Kierkegaard, has shown how this
self-centeredness of man is closely interwoven with man's anxiety.[11]
Man is a complex being; he is an animal among the animals, and
yet he is but a little lower than the angels. As Niebuhr puts it, man
is in nature and yet he continually transcends nature. Man continually transcends himself in that he can look at himself and ap-
prove or disapprove of what he sees. He can use his reason to find a
conclusion and then transcend his reason by asking if his reason
were adequate to deal with the problem. This situation of man results in anxiety because the transcendent aspect of man dreams
dreams, sets goals, finds meaning in life, sees that which makes life
worth living. But man's finite and natural self continually threatens
all the dreams and meanings of life, and thus man falls into anxiety
as he wonders if he can ever achieve what makes life worth living.

Man is everywhere a finite creature with boundaries beyond
which he cannot go. He may continually push back some of the
boundaries, such as the limits of knowledge, but he can never escape
them. The boundaries are, in the light of Christianity, the marks of
man's creatureliness. But man's transcendent nature always strives
to go beyond the boundaries. Thus man dreams of a perfect justice,
but in actual life he never achieves it. He catches the vision of a per-

fect love and a perfect friendship, but the loves and friendships that he actually achieves fall short of the ideal. Man longs for the truth, the whole truth, and nothing but the truth; but in actual fact at any moment his knowledge is strictly limited, and the whole truth, for that matter absolute certainty about anything, eludes him. Man dreams of the fulfillment of himself and his potentialities in the fullness of life, but death stands as the inevitable barrier that cuts off all lives short of such fulfillment. He dreams of being perfectly righteous, but his attainments always fall short of his dream.

Now this situation in which man's reach ever exceeds his grasp is by no means evil. From out of it arises his creativity. If man were content with his boundaries, he would stagnate. His societies would be as changeless as the beehive, and his personal attainments would not exceed those of a cow. But inevitably such a situation fills man with an underlying anxiety. Everything for which he lives, everything that makes life meaningful and abundant, is thrown into question. Man is thus haunted by the anxiety that life may lose its meaning and purpose. Change and decay in all around he sees and thus he anxiously seeks for something that changes not.

Anxiety is not to be identified with fear. A man may be afraid of this or that specific danger, and such fear can be overcome by an act of courage. But anxiety lies deeper than any particular fear, and when one fear is overcome a man's anxiety will spawn a new fear. If a man is afraid that he has cancer, he can go to a doctor and get an examination that will remove his fear. But the doctor has no way of removing his underlying anxiety that is expressed in the fear of death itself. For this anxiety is not caused by any particular threat; it arises from out of the nature of life itself.

Because man is haunted with anxious insecurity he seeks everywhere to find security. He demands that his state give him social security in more ways than one. The state must be strong enough to protect him from his enemies; it must protect him against unemployment, old age, disease, and physical incapacity. Labor unions no longer simply bargain for higher wages; they want pension schemes, sickness benefits, and a guaranteed annual wage. Every month Americans give generously to foundations seeking cures for various diseases in the restless search to find security from sickness.

Psychologists and psychiatrists have driven home to us how important it is to give the child security. The child needs the security of love and a harmonious home or he will be beset by neuroses. The older theme of allowing the child to express himself in freedom from discipline is being given up because we are told that such a child is driven into insecurity since he is never sure of what he can get away with.

Christianity has nothing to say against these legitimate demands of the human being, but we must see that man does not find the security for which he seeks. The state gives him security, and he begins to fear that its " socialism " is robbing him of his freedom and initiative. It builds bigger and better weapons to defend him against his enemies, and then he trembles at the thought of the war of annihilation. Big business becomes concerned with employee relations, hires psychologists, and makes the worker feel that he is " wanted " and that he " belongs," and the result is that the employee fears that he is becoming the " organization man." Man longs to be accepted and to find security, and when accepted he fears that he is lost in the " lonely crowd." And so we find the irony that after a generation dedicated to seeking for security, we are more, not less, anxious. This is evident in the vigorous sales of " tranquilizers," in the thousands who seek help with psychiatrists, clergymen, peace-of-mind books, and countless other devices.

This is not so strange as it may seem. Psychiatrists have long recognized the anxiety of the child who has no love, but many of them have overlooked the anxiety of the child who is loved. The point is that while the person who lacks the sources of security has an obvious source of anxiety, such a person has little to lose. But the person who has much has more to lose and may be more anxious. The child who is surrounded by love, who knows that he is accepted by his parents, is a child who has much to lose — a whole world of love. As Niebuhr points out, poverty is a threat to the rich but not to the poor. Man seeks in vain to overcome anxiety by amassing the means of security. The more he amasses the more he has to lose, and so we find that anxiety is more marked in rich

America than it is in many poor nations.

Man's anxiety is closely associated with his sense of freedom. E. Aubrey tells us that his twelve-year-old daughter suggested that man is the animal who has " if " in his vocabulary. It would be difficult to get a better description of man's uniqueness. Because man has the ability to transcend himself and the present moment, he can survey the future in terms of " if." He sees alternatives, and he has to choose one of them. He can look to the past and wail about what might have been IF only he had done otherwise than he did.

As he faces the future, man knows that the meaning of life is threatened not simply by the fact that he is finite and has boundaries, but also by the fact that he sins. It is no wonder that man continually clutches at theories of determinism, for such theories enable him to blame his shortcomings on the determining forces about him. And deterministic philosophies are never completely wrong because most of the boundaries that man faces are limitations upon his freedom. To a large extent man is what his environment has made him; his power of decision is limited on all sides by his own past, the race's past, and a host of given facts. And yet man cannot live by a philosophy of determinism, for within the boundaries of heredity and environment, he does make decisions, and when he makes them he knows that he has become responsible. And with responsibility comes further anxiety.

Anxiety is a mark of man's dignity; we might go so far as to say that it is the mark of being created in the image of God. If man could not transcend his boundaries in thought, hope, and dreams, he would be simply another animal. If man could not be anxious, he could not be creative, he could not have the responsibility that comes with decision. And man, as God created him, was intended to find the answer to his anxiety by trusting God. Jesus tells us not to be anxious about our lives; we are to trust God to fulfill them. (Matt. 6:25-34.) If we would allow God to become the center of our lives, trusting his ability to fulfill their meaning, to forgive their sin, we could turn our natural anxiety into creative living. But here is where man sins; he commits the original sin. He is not content to be a creature who trusts God for his security; he wants to be like God and build his own security, to fulfill his life. He eats the forbidden fruit because he is promised that this will make him like God; he builds his towers of Babel to the sky in order that he may be God himself.

Theoretically man has two sinful means of escaping anxiety. He may try to establish security by his own efforts or he may flee from anxiety by denying his transcendent nature and so live on the level of the animal alone. That is, he might accept his boundaries completely and not try to rise above them. But this second alternative does not really seem to be a live option. When man falls into what we call " brutal " behavior, he does not become like the brutes, but sinks lower. Thus man commits rape, but no animal does. The sensualist is not content merely to satisfy his sexual urges; he must " make conquests," seduce women to his way. That is, even the man who tries to live on the animal level alone finds that he is expressing self-centeredness.

When man commits the original sin of centering his life on himself, he inevitably sins against his neighbor; for if man is to build his own security, he finds that he must do it at the expense of his fellow men. In order to gain a sense of security he must be able to look down upon those who are less secure. Since it is impossible, as we have seen, for man to cure his anxiety, he has to settle for the next best, a relative security. And so man seeks to find a ledge upon which he can sit and thank God that he is not like the wretches who sit below him. He seeks power, knowledge, and even goodness to give him a ledge that brings a sense of superiority. He hides his eyes from the boundaries that encompass him and pretends that he has overcome them.

And so man, striving to gain a sense of security, uses his positions of authority to lord it over others. Parents try to relive their lives through their children and destroy the children in the process. Thinkers claim to have the truth, the whole truth, and nothing but the truth, and so they scorn the thinking of those who went before or of their contemporaries. And, perhaps most diabolical of all, men use their righteousness and their religion to give them a place from which they can thank God they are not as others. They assert that they have been saved while others have not, that they belong to the one true church, that they have the one true creed. Where the true love of God is gone, the true love of neighbor becomes impossible. The neighbor is no longer one to be served; he is to be used, however subtly, to bolster our own ego.

But few men can build individual ledges for themselves that give them a satisfactory sense of security. Man was created for dependence upon God, and where there is such dependence there is freedom from any institution or thing. Thus the Puritan absolutely submitted himself before God, but he laid the foundations of democracy because, being submitted to God, he had nothing left to submit to men, be they kings or dictators. But where men do not submit to God, their restless search for security results in their giving of themselves to a host of alternatives. Man who refuses to submit himself to God ends up in a grotesque parody of his God-relationship; he falls into idolatry. He worships the state, his race, his business organization, his labor union, his academic institution, and his church through all of which he gains his sense of superiority. These idols form the ledge upon which he sits to find his security. We do not understand racism, nationalism, or other such isms until we see how man uses his identification with the group to exalt himself and to satisfy his need to feel superior to others.

It is interesting to see how, in the earlier individualistic period of our nation, man's self-centeredness took the form of a Promethean pride. Man sought to be the rugged individualist; he was the " inner-directed man " of Riesman's analysis.[12] He did not care for public opinion; he rode roughshod to personal triumphs and found security in them. But the pattern has changed, and today man increasingly finds security, not in rugged egoism, but in group egoism. He becomes the " other-directed " person who seeks security through the prestige of his peer group.[13] The Promethean individual could be careless of public opinion because he was building his own security. But the other-directed individual becomes acutely conscious of the opinion of his peer group because his security depends upon his position within the group. The man who dares to be different is cast out in such an age because he rocks the ship of security in which men are sailing. Reinhold Niebuhr has said, " Emancipated from every reverence toward Him whose service is perfect freedom, the modern generation celebrated its brief hour of freedom and then capitulated to a variety of ridiculous tribal gods and political religions."

To the Christian, man's oscillation between Promethean " inner-directedness " and lonely " other-directedness " is a mark of sin. Man was created to be " God-directed." When he does not accept this he sinks into idolatry.

Because man's problem is self-centeredness, man cannot cure himself. For any act by which man would cure himself would be an act of the self and, instead of removing the self from the center, would entrench the self more firmly at a new level. We never fully see the problem of sin until we see how, as Niebuhr puts it, sin can use goodness as its vehicle of expression. When man the sinner screws up his energies, pulls on his bootstraps, and improves his moral life, or becomes religious, immediately he falls into the sin of the Pharisee and thanks God that he is not like those who have failed to improve their moral life. And so the most pernicious stronghold of sin is within the good life itself.

It should never be forgotten that in the Bible the chief competitor to God is never atheism, secularism, or vice. It is religion. In the Old Testament the prophets' chief problem is idolatry. In the New Testament it is the scribes and the Pharisees, the religious leaders, who are most opposed to Christ. Sinful man uses his goodness and his religion to exalt himself. Religion may be the point at which man finds true humility in the presence of God, but it may also be the point where he congratulates himself that he has God on his side.

When man seeks to exalt himself he puts himself into inevitable competition with his fellow man. He is not simply a greedy man who wants to be rich; he must be richer than others. As C. S. Lewis has pointed out, other sins are competitive only by accident, but pride is competitive by nature.[14] The self-centered man is not content to be good or to be religious; he must be better and more religious than someone else. His very security depends upon being able to thank God he is not like someone else. We all see and detest such behavior in others, but we see and detest it precisely because it makes them such serious competitors to our own need to feel superior.

The final absurdity is reached when, in a Christian culture, we become proud of our humility. We recall the all-too-true story of the church school teacher who, having taught the parable of the Pharisee and the publican, closed by saying, " Now, children, let us all thank God that we are not like the Pharisee."

In short, the self cannot cure itself of self-centeredness even by the seemingly radical act of self-denial. For immediately we become proud of ourselves for our heroic self-denials. We thank God that we are not like the people who indulge themselves. It is no wonder that Paul, when faced with the depths of the problem, cried out, " O wretched man that I am! who shall deliver me from the body of this death? " (Rom. 7:24).

VII.

Salvation

IN RECENT YEARS the most common charge hurled at the revivers of a reformation theology has been that they have concentrated upon sin and lost sight of salvation. As a result, it is claimed, these theologians see man as a sinner who can do nothing to save himself. They have cut the nerve of Christian ethical endeavor. Instead of attacking social and individual sins as liberalism did, these theologians are working out rationalizations that enable man to sit complacently in the midst of such sins. Paul Holmer, for example, recently made the charge that this theology is being used as an escape from ethical demands.[1]

If this charge is true, it is not surprising. We have seen that sin uses goodness and religion for its ends. We would expect that it will also use theology to justify itself. The Bible gets quoted to justify the antibiblical sin of racial discrimination. We need not be surprised to find that a theology that realistically analyzes sin is used by the very sin that it analyzes.

Furthermore, it must be admitted that as the realism of orthodox Christianity was recovered, the first emphasis was primarily upon man's sin. This was the particular need of the time. Reinhold Niebuhr quite rightly found in the thirties that modern man's chief characteristic was his complacent view of himself. Until this mask of complacency was torn from him, man could not understand the message of salvation. No one gets excited about a savior so long as he feels safe. But, although the critics do not seem to have realized it, the new reformation theology has moved from diagnosis to cure, from analysis of sin to a doctrine of salvation. No one has emphasized sin more than Karl Barth, and yet we find him saying, " Only the doer of the Word is its real hearer." [2] Furthermore, he asserts that no praise of God is serious if it does not include love of our neighbor.[3] Thus he concludes, "Dogmatics has no option: it has to be ethics as well." [4]

The Christian doctrine of salvation, however, is from beginning to end the gospel of what God has done for man. Christianity is always tempted to become a system of ethical ideals. This is a subtle compliment to man; it tells him that he is really very good, and can, if he will pull up his socks, do noble and wonderful things. But this is no cure. On the contrary, it fans the flame of self-righteousness or drives a man to despair.

When John Wesley rediscovered the Reformation in his day, his opponents charged him with spreading pessimism. A new reformation theology may well re-echo Wesley's answer. He said: "'If a man cannot be saved by all that he can do, this will drive men to despair.' True, to despair of being saved by their own works, their own merits or righteousness. And so it ought; for none can trust in the merits of Christ, till he has utterly renounced his own." [5]

The Christian doctrine of salvation is the doctrine of God's atoning work. Christianity is built on the fact of atonement. Through the life, death, and resurrection of Christ man finds that he has been made at one with God, that he is restored to the relationship with God for which he was intended. Apart from this fact there is no gospel. And yet it is interesting that Christianity has no orthodox doctrine of atonement to compare with its orthodox doctrine of the Trinity or the incarnation. In the history of the church three major doctrines have been held — the ransom theory for the first thousand years, the Anselmic and the Abelardian since that time.[6] Conservatives generally have insisted that only some form of the Anselmic (vicarious) atonement could be accepted, and liberals have insisted generally that only an Abelardian (moral influence) theory could do justice to the Christian faith.

It is strange that the ransom theory, which was the dominant theory for the first thousand years of Christianity, has been forgotten. Neither conservative nor liberal saw it as a live option. But the new reformation movement has restored interest in this traditional doctrine. Aulén may not have completely proved his case that this was *the* theory of atonement preached by Luther, but he certainly proves that this was an important element in Luther's theology. Even a casual reading of Luther's famous hymn, "A Mighty Fortress Is Our God," will reveal that. It is our thesis that a new reformation theology must seek to maintain the truth in each of the three traditional theories if it is to do justice to the full depths of the gospel.

The ransom theory, or the "classic" theory as Aulén calls it, is centered around the concept of the victory of Christ over the forces of evil. Man is pictured as owned, because of his sin, by Satan. Christ, the God-man, comes, and Satan thinking him to be an ordinary man, claims his life upon the cross. But Satan finds that he has taken that to which he has no right — the Son of God; he cannot hold Christ, so Christ is raised from the dead. Because Satan has taken that to which he had no right, he is found guilty of "false arrest" and must forfeit his claim upon sinners who accept Christ.

The obvious weakness of this theory is that it is put into a mythical framework, a framework that became more and more crude until Gregory the Great could speak of Christ's flesh as the bait used by God on his hook to catch the great leviathan, Satan. As such, the doctrine seemed to give Satan so much power that God had to pull a rather shady trick to win the battle. Furthermore, man was left as a spectator of a great cosmic drama; he was not an actor but the pawn over which supernatural forces battled.

But we should never allow the mythical elements in the doctrine to hide its truth. It has a great deal of support in the New Testament.[7] Better than any other doctrine it combines the incarnation, the cross, and the resurrection. It explains why Paul says that if Christ be not raised from the dead, we are still in our sins (I Cor. 15:17).

The ancient world could understand this doctrine because it had a deep sense of being caught and trapped by fate. The Stoic met this situation by counseling man to accept whatever fate might bring with *apatheia*. Man must be equally unconcerned whether he was happy or sad, wealthy or poor, an emperor or a slave. In the popular mind this sense of fate was expressed by saying that man was imprisoned by demonic forces that controlled his life. It is difficult for us to realize the great sense of relief that came to ancient man when he heard that the forces of evil, the demonic fates, had been defeated through Christ by God. Satan, sin, and death had lost their hold upon man. In Christ we are free. As a man is redeemed or ransomed from slavery or imprisonment, God has redeemed and ransomed mankind.

Today we live again in a world where this ancient theme takes on a new meaning. Modern man has a sense of being captured by fate, by powers beyond his control. He feels the tides of history bearing him, whether he will or no, to situations that he does not desire. Man feels lost and helpless as the world rushes forward to atomic destruction. Or the powers of fate may be seen in the scientific picture of a completely determined universe, so that man is predestined by forces over which he has no control. Or the powers of fate may take on a more demonic form, as they do in psychiatric theories of the subconscious. Deep within man's subconscious lie forces over which he has no control but which force their way into his consciousness and determine his acts. Or again, the controlling forces may appear in the form of the lonely crowd in which man as an individual is lost until finally he becomes so much of a moral chameleon that he no longer knows which of the selves he puts on display is his real self.

We find an understanding of this aspect of the world in contemporary literature, drama, art, and poetry. The demonic has come back to us in the distorted forms of modern art, and the broken language of the " underground " movement in poetry. Existentialist writers have held before us the mirror of our anxiety and meaninglessness. Jean-Paul Sartre follows his hero, Mathieu, through three long novels and shows him trying to perform one meaningful act, an act that will be truly free and hence the expression of his self. But everything Mathieu does is a conditioned act; he is pushed or pulled by this or that determining force. And finally, as the Germans overrun his country and his army unit is ordered to surrender, Mathieu performs his free act. He refuses to surrender and dies in a completely senseless gesture. His only free act is the meaningless act by which he throws life away. In short, the circle has come back to its starting point. With the Stoic of old, the modern existentialist is calling us to find meaning in defying the undefiable, resisting the irresistible.

In terms of our earlier analysis of sin we might say that modern man is experiencing the fear of his creatureliness. He senses that his boundary situations are closing in on him and that his spiritual life, what makes him a man, is being suffocated. The meaning of life seems to have been taken from his hands and to have no relationship to the fate that he must live.

To man in such extremities, and at the end of his tether, it is no good to preach moralism. Moral appeals will only make man more conscious of his incapacity. In such a situation man needs, above all else, the good news that his enemies have been defeated. He needs to know that the forces of fate and the demonic intruders into life do not have the last word. This is still God's world and God has within his hands the power to win the victory. God already has engaged the forces of evil in mortal combat and he has won. Christ is risen! History is not a " tale told by an idiot " that signifies nothing; it is the realm into which God has come and demonstrated his sovereign power. Once more our modern world can listen to Luther:

> " And though this world, with devils filled,
>   Should threaten to undo us;
> We will not fear, for God hath willed
>   His truth to triumph through us."

It is no accident that the ecumenical movement has made " Christ is Lord " its central proclamation. We need to know who is the Lord of this world in which we find ourselves. There is no good news in the gospel unless Christ is Lord over all that seems destined to crush our freedom, person, and independence. This is no simple success story; even Christ triumphs only through a cross. This is no facile promise that if we become Christian our troubles will cease. This is the deeper faith that enabled Paul to cry, " We are troubled on every side, yet not distressed; we are perplexed, but not in despair " (II Cor. 4:8).

The second great doctrine proposed by Anselm is that of vicarious atonement. This doctrine sees God as a God of love and of justice. Because of his justice God cannot simply forgive sinful man, for man's guilt makes him unacceptable to God. Man can do nothing to remove the guilt; he already owes all to God, so he can give God nothing to pay for his sin that he does not already owe to God. The only hope for man is that Christ, the God-man, takes man's punishment upon himself vicariously. Jesus is punished in our place. On the cross he bears the agonies of punishment, even to the point of being forsaken by God (Mark 15:34). Because our sin has been paid for, because punishment has been inflicted, God can now accept sinful man to himself.

This doctrine has many objectionable features. It drops the New Testament picture of the family relationship between God the Father and man the son, and puts into its place the picture of a law court. Man is the prisoner at the bar and God is the stern judge who will not let man go until the last pound of flesh is paid. Furthermore, although the doctrine claims to save the justice of God, it is difficult to see what is just about punishing one man for another's sin. As in the classic theory, man is left standing in the wings, watching celestial actors bargain over him. The doctrine is always in danger of picturing God's love and justice as separated. God the Father represents justice that must be propitiated and Christ represents love that will do the propitiating. And thus we lose the central emphasis of the New Testament that it is God who is in Christ, that atonement is the work of God from the beginning to the end. This doctrine has suffered also from crudely mythical elements as its exponents have fallen into orgies of talking about the "blood drawn from Immanuel's veins" into which sinners must be plunged if they would be clean. All of this comes more obviously from the Roman mystery cult of Mithra than from Christ.

But this doctrine also has its deep truth, or it would not have the power it most evidently does have. It certainly has a Biblical foundation.[8] The truth of this doctrine lies in the fact that it takes seriously the problem of guilt. It is no longer just the theologian and the moralist who are concerned with this problem. Today the physician and the psychiatrist know that guilt can actually make us ill. Man tries to ignore the fact of his guilt and thinks that he has got rid of it, but it sinks into his subconscious and there it festers until its poison creeps out to corrupt his whole nature.

Self-centered man always faces the problem of guilt. Because we love ourselves we want to be lovable selves; as we exalt ourselves we need to believe that we are worthy of exaltation. But none of us can live up to his ideal for himself. This creates a problem of guilt; man does not like himself; he cannot accept himself. It is a serious problem for the self-centered individual when his life is built around himself and yet he doesn't like his self.

It is significant that what the theologian often calls " inordinate self-love " and what the psychiatrist calls " self-hate " are really two sides of the same coin. Those who see here an irreconcilable contradiction have been hypnotized with words and failed to see the meanings involved. A man hates what he knows himself to be; that is the psychiatrist's point. But this is serious because the man's whole life is built around himself. That is, because in the theologian's terms he is filled with inordinate self-love. Similarly when the psychiatrist says that the man's need is to learn to love himself and the theologian says that his need is to cease to love himself, they are not necessarily opposed to each other. The two disciplines have different jargon.

If a person knows that he is extremely ugly, it will create the same psychological problems as if he knows that he is morally unacceptable. If this person is centered in himself, this physical ugliness will be a serious problem. Because, in theological language, he loves himself inordinately, he is unnerved and shocked by this lack of perfection in himself. He seeks to fulfill his life in himself, but his appearance mitigates against the fulfillment. He feels inferior beside other persons. He cannot accept what he is; he does not live up to his hopes for himself. Somehow this man must compensate, and he may do it by trying to rule over others and to exalt himself at their expense and prove his superiority. This is seen by the psychiatrist as " self-hate."

As the theologian sees it, this man needs to be freed from his self-love; he needs to be taken out of himself so that he can view himself with objectivity. When he no longer seeks to fulfill his life's meaning within himself and by his own power, he can accept his own ugliness and even laugh at it.

The same principle applies when man finds that his actions fall short of his moral ideals. (And every man finds this.) Because he builds his life around himself, he is dismayed to find that his self is not worthy of the love that he showers on it. And so man, as sinner, has to seek to escape from the tension of knowing himself to be unworthy. He may try to compensate for this by asserting himself more belligerently in other ways. He seeks to have power over individuals so that he can assure himself of superiority over them. Such a man cannot love his neighbors; he has to use them to bolster up his sagging self-esteem. He may become the ruthless " self-made " man. He may become the well-known figure of the reformer who so loves all mankind that he works incessantly to save mankind but who hates every individual whom he meets. He may become a tyrant in his home or office. He may become a religious zealot, fiercely denouncing the sins of other men, especially the " sins " that he does not commit — smoking, dancing, drinking, etc.

Along with the foregoing, or perhaps instead of them, he will find other defenses against the realization of his guilt. A most useful dodge is the " everybody is doing it " line. (How we loved the Kinsey reports!) No matter how sinful I am, 64.5 per cent of the American males are worse. When we fall below our ideal for ourselves, we can either strive anew to meet the ideal or we can pull the ideal down to our attainments. The latter is easier. And so Christianity gets reduced to " respectable " living. We meet the minimum moral demands of our society and thank God that we are not like those who fall below respectability.

If none of these defenses against our guilt will work, we will fall into despair. This may take the extreme form of suicide, but more normally it takes the form of neurosis: the guilt-driven individual escapes into alcoholism, restless busyness, or even physical illness.

When first we approach the gospel, it seems to be bad news because everyone of our defenses against guilt is torn down. We are faced with an ethical demand higher than any social mores. It is no answer to God to say that our neighbor is worse than we are. We have prided ourselves on our guilt complex, but when we face God we know that our problem is not a guilt complex; our problem is that we are guilty. And so man is driven to despair, a more radical despair than any that secular man can know. There is nothing to do but to confess, "I am by nature sinful and unclean." Wherever the demands of God are taken seriously, they lead to despair. This is seen in the early lives of Paul, Luther, and Wesley.

This is why the Christian faith should never be presented simply as a moral ideal. If Christianity is made to seem a way of life that we must live, it will drive us to despair or to water down the Christian ethic to equal respectable living. Christianity is gospel first and demand second. First it comes to us with the assurance that our guilt is gone. God has not found us righteous, nor has he pretended that our sins do not matter; but God has taken our guilt and borne it upon himself. "While we were yet sinners, Christ died for us." (Rom. 5:8.)

When a man has been unfaithful to his wife and longs to atone, he comes home bearing gifts to make up for what he has done. But no gift can pay the price. The harm done to the love relationship cannot be repaired even by a new fur coat. The relationship is restored only by the wife's bearing in her heart the ache and the pain of accepting the husband back. Thus God is not the stern judge who cannot allow the law to be broken; he is the righteous father who bears the full penalty of guilt for his prodigal son.

The doctrine of vicarious atonement has preserved a truth that must be experienced by every Christian. He has stood guilty before the Holy and Righteous God, and yet in the moment that he stood defenseless there, the burden of sin has fallen from him, as it fell from Bunyan's pilgrim when he stood before the cross. This leaves man free to face the fact of his guilt. He does not need to force it into his subconscious where it will fester; he can bring it out into the open and know that even as it is faced, it is gone. The man who continues to berate himself for his past sins is the man who lacks faith in the sovereignty of God's love. Because man knows that he is accepted by God, he can accept himself. And because he no longer is filled with self-judgment, he is freed from the defense of judging others. He can love his neighbor.

The third doctrine of atonement, first proposed by Abelard, is known as the moral-influence theory. Basically it affirms that God is a Father who is always willing to forgive his erring children. But forgiveness is not something that can be unilateral. If my friend begins to injure me, I cannot forgive him in the sense of restoring him to the former relationship of friendship, unless he wishes to be restored. I can condone his actions, but I cannot forgive them. And so, it is argued, God is always willing to forgive; but so long as man prefers the riotous living in the far country, or even his life in the pigsty, there can be no forgiveness. Man must repent; he must desire to be restored to the true relationship with God.

And so, said Abelard, God sent his Son to live the perfect life in contrast to which man sees his sin. In Christ God shows man that he loves him, and when the Son of God goes to the cross man sees this love burning at white heat. Face to face with this love, man's sinful heart melts and he repents. That is, the cross does not effect a change in God's relationship to man; it changes man's attitude toward God.

By itself, this theory is weakest where the other two are strongest. God, having acted, leaves the initiative to man. Man hears no good news that the forces of evil have been defeated, that his guilt has been lifted from him. Furthermore, it is often argued, since this theory sees no objective reason for Christ's death, it cannot be a means of moving man to repentance. If I am drowning and a man jumps in to save me, I know that he loves me. But if I am safe on the bank and he jumps into the water, saying, " See how I love you," it proves nothing. In other words, to have a moral influence upon man, the cross needs to be more than a moral influence.

On the other hand, this theory is strongest where the others are weakest. It does not see atonement as a drama that man watches from the reserved seats. Man is involved. " Were you there when they crucified my Lord? " Yes, I am there now; the cross speaks to me and I turn to accept it. There is solid Scriptural basis for this doctrine also.[9]

The moral-influence theory expresses the truth that atonement works a real change in man. Psychiatrists tell us that a man cannot love until he has been loved. I think theology can see why. Man, self-centered, seeking to justify himself, is too concerned with the self to love another truly. To love we have to cease to be the center of our self. In love a person is pulled out of himself. Nothing is more self-centered than a newborn child; his world is built around himself completely. But when the child is in the midst of a loving home, he is pulled out of himself. Because others love him, he loves in return. This we see on the purely natural level, but such natural love is always limited. The more we love our families the less we love those who threaten our families.

When the Christian sees Christ going to the cross for him, he knows that he is loved with a love transcending every human love. And because he is loved, he can love in return. Sometimes Christianity is preached as self-denial. But that is a perversion. Nothing is more unlovely than the man who self-righteously denies himself. The Christian way is not self-denial; it is self-forgetfulness. But the self cannot forget itself by any act of its own. We really forget ourselves only when we love. The man who has never thought of anyone else's pleasure or comfort falls in love and suddenly his life has a new center; now he finds true happiness in making another person happy. He has forgotten himself. And so the moral influence theory is an indispensable part of the truth of atonement. In the cross we know that God loves us, and this knowledge pulls us out of ourselves so that we love God in return. And he who loves God will love his neighbors whom God loves.

This analysis of atonement leads straight to the central Reformation doctrine — salvation by grace through faith. The Christian is a man who has realistically faced his weakness, who knows that he is not worthy of standing before God. He has ceased fooling himself and has accepted the fact of his unacceptableness. He knows that by no act of his own can he make himself a righteous and loving individual. If man remained self-centered, this would drive him to utter despair. But when he knows with this the loving grace of God, he ceases to be concerned with himself.

As Luther pointed out so profoundly in his lectures on Romans, the very mark of the " saved " man is that he is willing to be damned if God should will it. The saints are those who love God so completely that they would be prepared to go to hell for his sake. (Rom. 9:3.) The truly damned, said Luther, are those who fear and flee from damnation. Calvin made the same point when he affirmed that the Christian was content to be predestined to damnation for the glory of God. We can see how far the Protestant Church has moved from the Reformation when it becomes in many of its forms an agency to save men from hell or personal discomforts. A church that centers man's attention on the question " Are you saved? " has betrayed the Reformation and it has betrayed Christ. When God's grace really grips us, we lose all concern about whether we have been saved. " For whosoever will save his life shall lose it." (Luke 9:24.)

Man is brought to this selfless love only where he knows that he is loved, where he loves in response to One who first loved him. Salvation by grace means that our relationship to God depends first of all upon God and not upon ourselves. Instead of looking at the state of our souls to see how they are doing in the religious life, we look to God and what he has done. As a child is born into a family and is loved irrespective of his desserts or attainments, so man is loved by God irrespective of his value to God.

Here lies the Reformation basis for infant Baptism. It is significant that the Anabaptist wing of the Reformation rejected infant Baptism completely. Many exponents of a new reformation theology, including Barth and Brunner, have raised serious questions about the validity of infant Baptism. Protestantism cannot accept any view of Baptism as a semimagical act which saves man from sin or gives him a ticket for heaven. When Protestantism denies salvation by works, it not only means that man cannot save himself by his works, but it also means that the church cannot save him by its works either. There is only one justification for infant Baptism. It is the symbolic act in which it is affirmed that before we ever thought of seeking God, he had sought us. Before we were able to lift a finger to deserve it, God's love had claimed us. God had elected us already to his grace. When the day came that we attained to the age of decision and accepted God, it was not some bright new idea of ours, but was a step for which God had been working since our birth.

But man is not saved like a chess pawn being moved. Although his salvation begins with God's action, it comes before him with a challenge to which he must respond. His response is faith. We have said much about faith already; here we are looking at it in terms of salvation. We have argued that faith is not to be equated with beliefs. When speaking about salvation it is most important to remember this. If faith becomes a belief, then it is a work that we perform to earn our salvation. Where Protestantism has perverted faith into a belief in doctrines, it has offered a cheap substitute for salvation. Faith is not a belief-work; it is a response to the love of God. Salvation is a person-to-person relationship between God and man. Faith is man's acceptance of this relationship, his entry into it.

This is why, as Emil Brunner says, the rite of confirmation is necessary to restore the New Testament emphasis on man's response in Baptism. In Baptism the infant can make no response to the grace of God extended to him. But we do not become Christians by proxy. The day must come when we make our own decision and choice, when we accept for ourselves the promises made to us in Baptism. This is not to say that every Christian must undergo a dramatic conversion experience, but it is to say that, as Gordon Allport puts it, we cannot inherit our religion as we inherit the family jewels. Faith implies commitment, and sooner or later man must make the decision that commits him to or against God. The man who is confronted by God in Christ, who knows that in his Baptism God's love surrounded him, responds to God's grace with his faith.

But if we are to understand the Christian faith, we must see that it is always and only faith in God. Will Herberg has argued that the typical American has faith in faith.[10] I believe that this is true; we have faith in what our faith can do for us. But the Christian does not have faith in man, not even in man's faith. He has faith in God alone.

An analogy can show why faith in faith is wrong. A loving relation between persons always involves faith or trust. If a man hires a private detective to follow his wife to see if she is faithful to him, the marriage is already broken, even if the detective finds her innocent, because when trust goes out of a marriage the love relation has been broken. But there is a more subtle way of destroying the relationship. It is for the man to say, in effect, " I trust you; therefore, you would not dare betray my trust." That is, he does not have faith in his wife; he has faith that his faith will force her to behave herself. Many a person tries to manipulate another person by using love and trust as a tool to compel the other to do his will.

In religion we are continually tempted to use our faith as a lever to manipulate God. In effect, we say to God, " You could not reject me when I have such perfect faith in you." A mark of a sick Protestantism is always to be seen when the Protestant begins looking at himself and finding comfort in some act of his own, even the act of faith, instead of looking to God.

Many Christians are prone to examine themselves to see whether they are holding the right theology or having the right religious experiences. And when they are not busy at that, they are busy judging their neighbors. But a thoroughgoing Protestantism knows that to be saved by grace means that I can never find within myself the assurance of my salvation. It means that I have security in God alone. To trust God fully and completely means to trust God to complete even the weak faith that we offer to him. " I believe; help thou mine unbelief." (Mark 9:24.)

An alcoholic once told me how he had been saved from his alcoholism by his Christian faith. But he marveled at how long he had stayed away from God. It was only when he had dragged himself and his family to the point where they hit, as he put it, " rock bottom," that he turned to God. And as he analyzed it, he said that what had held him back was his desire to be worthy of God before he came to him. That man was saying what Protestant theologians are trying to say. We want to be worthy *before* we come to God so that we can deserve what he will do for us. Our self-love drives us to make ourselves worthy, and so we cling to a doctrine of salvation by works.

If it were true that the exponents of a new reformation theology had a doctrine of grace as forgiveness alone, it would be a betrayal of the Reformation. For while the Reformers knew that man is justified, accepted by God, regardless of his lack of good works, they also asserted with Paul that justification leads to sanctification, the new life in Christ. This was the truth that Wesley saw with particular clarity. Justification may occur quickly as a man sees God's forgiving love and surrenders to it. But sanctification, the growth in the Christian life, is a lifelong task. Turning to God does not immediately banish from a man's life his sins; it does not immediately break down his past habits. Furthermore, because it is through faith that we are saved, our anxiety is never completely overcome. We still long to get a hold upon God to give ourselves security. It is no accident that the closer men come to God, the more deeply they are aware of their sin. Pascal was correct when he asserted that there are only two classes of persons, the sinners who think that they are righteous and the righteous who know that they are sinners.

The Protestant has lost one motive to do good — the motivation based on a system of rewards and punishments. He knows that he cannot be good enough to earn salvation or to escape damnation. He knows that his ultimate destiny has nothing to do with whether or not he has been good. He knows that our final pay will not be proportioned to the amount of work we have done in the vineyard. (Matt. 20:1-16.) To many people this seems like the death of ethical living. Even many groups that claim to live by salvation through faith cannot act upon this principle. By actual rules or social pressures they force their members to obey certain moralistic codes. It is difficult to trust God and God alone for our salvation.

But psychological experiments have demonstrated that motivations to action based on fear or hope of reward are usually weak. Safety groups have drilled us in the fundamental truths that " Speed kills," " The life you save may be your own," but this does not seem to have affected the accident rate on our roads. Furthermore, moral philosophers are almost universally agreed that the lowest form of ethical motivation is that which is based on reward and punishment. Therefore, when Protestantism rejects this motivation it has not lost a particularly compelling motive or one that is morally worth keeping.

But if the Protestant has lost the motive of reward and punishment, he has a new and stronger motivation. Instead of being good to save himself here or hereafter, the Protestant is called to live the Christian life out of gratitude for what God *has done* for him. So long as Luther was striving to save himself by his own good works in the monastery, his feverish question was, "What is the *least* I must do to save myself?" When he learned the truth of salvation through grace, he changed his question to "What is the *most* I can do for the God who has done everything for me?"

But the Christian is not simply moved by gratitude. He is called into a loving relationship with God. A man will do some things from a sense of fear, he will do more from a sense of duty, and still more from a sense of gratitude. But he will do most where he loves. When we have to be reminded of our duty to someone whom we love, our love already has lagged in its zeal. When a young man takes flowers to his girl friend, he does not do it because he is afraid not to, nor because it seems to be his duty; he does it simply because it will please her. Where we truly love, the strongest motivation of all is the motivation to please the one we love. When Augustine said that we are to love God and do as we please, he was not giving a license for immorality; he was pointing to the strongest moral motivation of all. He who truly loves God will wish to do that which will please God.

No one has understood this fact more profoundly than Luther. In fact, Luther emphasized that whenever we have a sense of ought, or duty, we have already fallen into sin. He was right. We only experience the sense of duty where there is a disinclination in us to do something. When we are doing as we please, we never stop to think that this is our duty. The man who is in the proper relationship with God does not need the sense of ought, or duty. But if Luther understood most profoundly the nature of love, Calvin saw that we cannot leave behind the sense of duty because we never do attain the proper relationship with God. But when the Christian reminds himself of his duty, he does it in the presence of the One whom he loves. The burden of duty has become light because it is in the context of love.

Earlier we argued that revelation presents to us its own criteria by which it is to be judged. One of those criteria was its ability to fulfill its own promises. A major promise of the New Testament is that we will be new men in Christ. We can now see its meaning in the light of a doctrine of salvation. The Christian finds a new source of ethical power in his relationship with God through Christ. He finds that the forces that have prevented him from loving his neighbor are broken down, that he is freed to love. We believe the Christian revelation because we have experienced in our own lives the renewal of moral power that Christ has promised us. (II Cor. 5:17.)

But we should emphasize what kind of proof this is. This is not an objective proof to persuade the unbeliever. An unbeliever may be moved to look farther into Christianity by the moral strength that he finds in some Christian. But the Christian's moral strength will prove nothing unless the unbeliever comes to find new strength in his own life. Furthermore, there is no way of examining statistically the moral habits of Christians and showing objectively that they are better than those of the unbelievers.

There are several reasons why a statistical proof cannot be made. For one thing, only God knows who the Christians are and hence who should be included on the Christian side of the statistics. Secondly, we can never suppose that in morality we all begin together from the starting line as in a foot race. Our heredity and environment stamp us deeply, and everyone begins the moral race with a particular handicap. Therefore, the actual attainment of a man never tells how much his religion has aided him. Finally, if the Christian claimed that he was enough better than the unbeliever to prove anything, he would fall into the worse sin of thanking God that he was not like the unbeliever.

This confirmation, like all confirmations of revelation, is not an objective proof. It can be, in the nature of the case, a proof only to the believer himself. I can never say that, as a Christian, I am better than some unbeliever. What I can say is that I am better *than I would be* without Christ. Once more let us remember that we cannot prove ourselves righteous by looking at our neighbors. We are not to be judged by the standard of our neighbor; we are judged by the standard of Christ. And so we can judge ourselves only by Christ. We can confess that we have come closer to the ideal of Christ through God's grace than we could have done on our own power. This is a confirmation of the gospel that each Christian can find in his own life. And this is a witness that he can make. Such witnessing is not boasting. On the contrary, for any Christian to pretend that his present moral attainment is of his own doing would be the height of arrogance. What we are may not be much, but it would be much less without the grace of God.

No discussion of salvation would be complete without emphasizing the social implications of the Christian life. Unfortunately I do not have space here to dwell on this theme. I have devoted a book elsewhere to this subject, and if anyone would argue that I have slighted the social application, I would refer to it.[11]

I would like to say a few words to the charge often heard that the revival of reformation theology has undercut the social concern of the churches. I believe that there has been a decline of social passion in recent years in church circles as compared to the days when liberalism was dominant. The extent of the decline is difficult to judge, however, as the social emphasis under liberalism seldom got down to the rank-and-file members of the church. But I do not believe that this decline can be charged to the new theology. The decline of social interest is even more marked between the two periods on the college campuses where it cannot be blamed on theology.

There are many reasons for a decline in social activism. A major reason is that men are bewildered by the complexities of our problems. What is the solution to the problem of war? It is not easy to say; we have seen too many pat answers fail in recent years. The present college generation is being called the "uncommitted generation," but the persons calling it that come from the overly committed generation of the thirties when everyone had a solution to the world's ills in his hip pocket. It is significant that there is one notable exception to the lack of social concern in both the colleges and the churches. That is on the race question, on which both colleges and churches have continued to express themselves forcibly.

But the race question is the one major social ill where we seem to be making some progress and where people can feel that they do see some real answers.

However we explain the lack of social concern, a new reformation theology must deplore it. Everything that we have said about sanctification has its social implications. The Christian, captured by the love of God in Christ, is drawn to love his neighbor as himself. But political, economic, and social relations deeply affect the neighbor. If he is crushed by racial discrimination, political tyranny, or economic injustice, the Christian cannot pass by on the other side. He must tackle the political and social structures that work this evil.

We live in an age caught between the major dangers of communism and atomic warfare. The church has not given leadership at this point. Its pronouncements have done little more than bless the prevailing political moods from whichever side of the Iron Curtain it has spoken. We might take satisfaction in the fact that, if the churches have failed, so have the scientists, newspapers, labor unions, and educational institutions. But the church has no right to take satisfaction by pointing to the sins of others. What is needed is a true repentance and a humble confession that we " have sinned, and come short of the glory of God." But a true repentance implies a willingness to do differently in the future. It may sound good, but it is of little help to man if we verbally repent while we calmly watch mankind disintegrate in atomic smoke.

The Christian's citizenship is in heaven; he has been claimed by God. But God has placed him in this world, and it is only here that he can at present serve God. There is a tension here; there always has been for the Christian. But it should be a creative tension. The Christian has a perspective from which he can speak to the moral, political, and social life of his time. This perspective always includes judgment; it finds that man and his institutions fall short of their destiny in Christ. But it is also a perspective of hope, for Christ has come. History A.D. is qualitatively different from history B.C. The judgment and the hope should both be held before the eyes of modern man. A theology that is true to the Reformation will proclaim both.

VIII.

Conclusion

THE THEOLOGICAL TASK is central to the life of the church. The first purpose of the church is to proclaim to the world the message that it has received. This proclamation occurs in preaching, teaching, the sacraments, and in deeds of love and mercy. The church's primary task is not its own self-preservation or glorification; it is the proclamation of the good news that has gripped it and upon which it lives and is nourished. Theology is the discipline through which the church continually re-examines its proclamation. A church that lost concern with theology would be a church that no longer cared what it said and did or why.

It is most important that the church continue to debate its theology. Theological debate is not a sign of deplorable division; it is a sign of a living church that cares enough about its God-given task to agonize over how well it is performing that task. Battles have been fought over one iota in the creed because the church was aware that its task was so vital that it could not afford to be careless of even an iota. We must avoid the kind of tolerance that, as Barth reminds us, means simply being so unconcerned about other persons that we are willing to leave them to their fate.[1] The church may have more important things to do than to think theologically, but if its theology is inadequate, it will find that its work on all fronts is hampered. One of the greatest contributions of the new reformation movement has been to force the church to face again its ultimate theological presuppositions.

The church has a gospel to proclaim to the world. In that task is implied a continual tension. There is a gospel to proclaim, and there is a world to which it is to proclaim it. The gospel is unchanging, but the world is in continual change. As a result the church has oscillated between two errors. At one time it forgets that it is called to speak to the world in which it finds itself; it repeats the theology of its fathers, and thus becomes irrelevant to the world in which it finds itself. The other danger is that, reacting against the former error, it identifies itself with its age and forgets that it has a gospel to proclaim. Both errors make the church impotent.

The peculiar danger of fundamentalism and conservatism is that, in their concern to keep the purity of the faith, they lose contact with the world. They repeat the theological thought-forms of another day and bemoan the sinful generation in which they find themselves. They try to turn the clock back to an age that nostalgia portrays as more congenial to the faith. They find themselves caught in a pathetic and hopeless battle with the science and general thought-forms of the age. Christianity is made to seem obscurantist, archaic, and outdated.

The conservative danger gives rise to the reaction that is the peculiar danger of the liberal, who, determined to be up to date, accepts the modern world and its thought-forms. But in his passion to be modern he loses the gospel. He is so concerned to speak to his age that he comes to the point where he has nothing to say to the world that the world is not already saying to itself and probably saying better. In his own way the modernist becomes as irrelevant as the fundamentalist. The fundamentalist has something to say to his world, but he has lost the ability to say it. The modernist knows how to speak to his age, but he has nothing to say.

Of course we are not saying that all conservatives commit the one error and all liberals the other. The best representatives of both schools have evaded both errors. And ironically, the conservative often commits the error of modernism and the liberal the error of conservatism. The new conservative theology of today, in its desire to be up to date, intellectual, and relevant, is in grave danger of conforming too closely to the modern age to be able to bring a word to that age. It finds itself so bound to Madison Avenue advertising techniques in its evangelism, so wedded to the social *status quo* in American life, that the eternal gospel becomes lost in a modern culture religion. And the liberal, as W. M. Horton has indicated, may accommodate himself so well to the modern world that, when the world changes, he is unable to change with it and sounds as quaintly out of date as the fundamentalist in another age. And so a liberal theologian may order the waves of contemporary philosophy to recede while he defends an idealism or Whiteheadianism that was up to date a generation ago.

The new reformation theology has the advantage of being warned by both dangers in our age. We have seen Christianity made into both an archaic world view and an emotional tinge to modernity. It is the hope and prayer of the new reformation theology that it may sail between the Scylla and the Charybdis of these twin dangers. The fact that it is a *new* reformation theology means that it sees the need to speak to the age in which it finds itself. No matter how much it learns from Calvin, Luther, or Wesley, it cannot speak their truth in their words to this century. But the fact that it is a new *reformation* theology means that it is looking with the Reformers to the Word that God has spoken to all times.

Ever since Barth's clarion call in his *Romans,* the prophecies that this new movement cannot last have been heard. Conservatives have seen it as the last gasp of a dying liberalism. Liberals have branded it as a pessimistic reaction to our time of troubles that will blow away with the dawn of more normal times. In recent years this has changed to the claim that neo-orthodoxy has passed away already. I think that we might accept this latter claim. What neo-orthodoxy means to most people has gone, if it ever existed. If neo-orthodoxy means, as its stereotype implies, an irrational theology that holds a pessimistic doctrine of sin without an adequate doctrine of grace, and has no concern with social problems, then we can gladly admit that it has passed. (We must add that we are unable to see that it ever existed except in the imagination of its critics.) But if we think of a new reformation theology as the movement that has won again the truths of the Reformation for our time, then the movements that are supposed to be replacing neo-orthodoxy are themselves expressions of the new reformation concern.

Many changes in the movement are due to its success, not to its failure. When Barth and Niebuhr first spoke their prophetic protests, they spoke to a world that was drunk with optimism and bloated with the pride of reason. If these men have changed their emphasis to a more optimistic and rational form, it is because they have won the battle they first fought and have moved to meet challenges from a new source. It is like Jeremiah who, before the Babylonian exile, preached a message of almost unmitigated gloom, but, immediately after the fall of Jerusalem, became the prophet of hope, promising that the people would return. Jeremiah's faith had not changed; the world to which he spoke had changed. Because his first prophecy had been fulfilled, he could sound a new note.

The real crisis that faces a new reformation theology today is not that it is decaying; its crisis arises from its obvious success. Precisely because its chief opponents are on the defensive, because it is even now taking over some of the last strongholds of its opposition, the movement is faced with the danger of complacency and success.

A great danger of the movement is that, in its concern to regain the treasures of orthodoxy, it will fall into sterile dogmatism. Elated by the rediscovery of the lost treasures, we are sorely tempted to feel spiritually secure because we believe that we are theologically correct. We thank God that we are not like the poor liberal who does not know that pride is man's original sin. We need to listen to Karl Barth reminding us that " Jesus Christ can and means to and will acknowledge in some sort of way, and that a wholesome and victorious way, even a church with a bad dogmatics and proclamation. . . ." [2] If theological correctness is made into an end in itself, it can become a serious block to the living Word of God, and at such a moment God must speak as he has spoken in similar situations, through those whose theology is not " correct."

But the most serious danger is that of supposing that we have a " correct " theology. This is a paradoxical danger, for the heart of the movement is its recognition of the Lordship of God and of our total dependence upon him. But it is nonetheless real. Even the theology that teaches that God can never be captured in a theology will be tempted to think that it controls God in this insight. Once again it is Barth who sees the danger. He says:

"I am thinking of a certain assurance of voice, speech, and attitude, with which, it appears, we can work . . . ; of a certain confidence with which we think we can take these mighty concepts
upon our lips, analyze them, and unite them constructively one to
the other, this way or that; of a certain sprightliness with which
we speak of the things signified by these concepts, as though we
spoke about them, because we know how to speak above
them . . . ; an assurance, certainty, and sprightliness which perhaps becomes but the greater, as we are clever enough also to work
in the element of uncertainty or of 'confident despair.' . . . Even
the most zealous theological treasure-hunting is certainly mere
folly apart from that 'being rich toward God' (Luke 12:21) which
no one can manufacture for himself or maintain for himself." [3]

The theological movement that has rediscovered the Reformation
truth that we are never morally good enough to win God's favor,
must not forget that theologically we are never correct enough to do
so either. In thought, as in morality, we are saved by grace and
grace alone.

Fosdick points out that in his experience with seminary students
he found that those who came to the new movement through liberalism often revealed insights into the Christian faith for which he
was grateful. But among those who had come into the new movement without a vital experience of liberalism, he found the worst
homiletical arrogance that he ever saw at Union Theological Seminary.[4] These words from the greatest of the liberals should sober
us, for an increasing number of our seminarians are cutting their
first theological teeth on the new reformation theology without a
prior experience of liberalism. A man like Fosdick, who still bears
the scars of having fought for theological freedom and personal integrity, knows full well that whatever the weakness of liberalism,
it fought a battle for the cause of Christ that must be fought again
in each theological generation.

All of this is to remind us of the need for continual theological
discussion and debate. I have been happy to participate in this series
in which three live options in theology today are presented. Because
theology is a most crucial task of the church, we must never allow

any one school of theology to reign. In recent years we have heard a great deal about the desirability of an ecumenical theology. Without denying the need and value of ecumenical theological discussion, I must confess a real fear of attaining an ecumenical theology. The very concept implies that finite men can gain the one true theology and, presumably, all deviators would be cast out into the unecumenical darkness. Theology is far too important to the church to make ecumenical agreement a chief end. The value of ecumenical discussion lies in the fact that there is not an ecumenical theology, and consequently each theology must continually question itself in the light of the challenge made to it by opposing positions.

Even the man who is most loyal to the orthodox tradition of the church must remember the debt that orthodoxy owes to heresy. Without the rise of heresy, orthodoxy might never have been formulated. Would we still remember Athanasius if he had not been challenged by Arius? How much less would have been the contribution of Augustine if he had not been stimulated by Pelagius and the Donatists! Would we still recall the obscure monk, Martin Luther, if medieval Rome had not fallen so deeply into heresy? If we could manage, by compromise and lukewarm zeal, to build an ecumenical theology, no matter how "correct," God would have to raise up new "heretics" to challenge the new idolatry.

In this book I have witnessed, to the best of my ability, to the theological convictions that have gripped me. I dare not hope that the result bears any theological finality, and I rejoice that this book will appear with the defense of alternative positions. If our joint efforts can play some part in reminding the church of the central need to reconsider its theological basis and force it to face the need of making a theological decision, I shall be more than happy.

If there is one aspect of the new reformation theology that stands out with peculiar cogency to me, it is this: our relationship to God is first and above all the result of God's activity, not of ours. In the God-man relationship, man brings only his finiteness, his sin, and his need. As a result, man never possesses God in his church, his creed, or his theology. But the wonder is that God takes what man has to offer, and, in his loving grace, he works his will even through man's

" earthen vessels " (II Cor. 4:7). Because we do not possess God we cannot pretend that our theological systems are more than finite and fallible efforts. But because we live by the grace of God we speak because we have the faith that God can and will use even these efforts.

NOTES

I. Challenge and Response in Twentieth-Century Theology

1. For a more extensive summary of each of these movements, see my book, *A Layman's Guide to Protestant Theology*. The Macmillan Company, 1955.

2. See Emil Brunner and Karl Barth, *Natural Theology*, tr. by P. Fraenkel. Geoffrey Bles, Ltd.: The Centenary Press, London, 1946.

3. See especially their comments on each other's positions in the volumes edited by Charles W. Kegley and Robert W. Bretall: *The Theology of Paul Tillich*. The Macmillan Company, 1952; and *Reinhold Niebuhr: His Religious, Social and Political Thought*. The Macmillan Company, 1956.

4. Morton White, *The Age of Analysis*, p. 174. Mentor Books, 1955.

5. John Hick, *Faith and Knowledge*, p. 138. Cornell University Press, 1957.

6. *Ibid.*, p. 139.

7. J. V. L. Casserley, *The Christian in Philosophy*, p. 168. Charles Scribner's Sons, 1951.

8. A. J. Ayer and others, *The Revolution in Philosophy*, pp. 75–76. The Macmillan Company, London, 1957.

9. Karl Barth, *Church Dogmatics*, Vol. I, Pt. 1, *The Doctrine of the Word of God*, tr. by G. T. Thomson, pp. 2–3. Charles Scribner's Sons, 1936.

10. J. Hick, *op. cit.*, p. v.

11. Basil Mitchell, editor, *Faith and Logic*, p. 2. George Allen and Unwin, Ltd., London, 1957.

II. Faith and Reason

1. See L. Harold DeWolf, *The Religious Revolt Against Reason*. Harper & Brothers, 1949.

2. M. J. Heinecken, *The Moment Before God*, pp. 41–42. Muhlenberg Press, 1956.

3. K. Barth, *Church Dogmatics,* Vol. I, Pt. 1, pp. 231 ff.

4. *Ibid.,* p. 153.

5. L. Harold DeWolf, *A Theology of the Living Church,* p. 37. Harper & Brothers, 1953.

6. There is an obvious similarity between my terms and the scholastic distinction of *notitia, fiducia,* and *assensus.* But the differences are so significant that I prefer to use somewhat different terms.

7. E. H. Sugden, editor, *Standard Sermons of John Wesley,* Vol. I, p. 40. Epworth Press, London, n.d.

8. Gustaf Aulén, *The Faith of the Christian Church,* p. 23. Muhlenberg Press, 1948.

9. *Ibid.,* p. 24.

10. K. Barth, *Church Dogmatics,* Vol. I, Pt. 2, tr. by G. T. Thomson and H. Knight, p. 172. Charles Scribner's Sons, 1956.

11. *Ibid.,* p. 26.

12. *Ibid.*

13. E.g., see M. C. Beardsley, *Practical Logic,* pp. 105–112. Prentice-Hall, Inc., 1950.

14. E.g., see J. Hospers, *An Introduction to Philosophical Analysis,* pp. 359–365. Prentice-Hall, Inc., 1953.

15. F. De Sua, "Consistency and Completeness," *The American Mathematical Monthly,* Vol. 63, No. 15, p. 305. May, 1956.

16. Victor Kraft, *The Vienna Circle,* pp. 143–144. Philosophical Library, Inc., 1953.

17. Richard Von Mises, *Positivism: A Study in Human Understanding,* p. 142. George Braziller, Inc., 1956.

18. John Hutchison, *Faith, Reason, and Existence,* p. 106. Oxford University Press, 1956.

19. R. M. Hare has argued this point half humorously in terms of what he calls a man's "blik." See Flew and MacIntyre, editors, *New Essays in Philosophical Theology,* pp. 99–103. The Macmillan Company, 1955.

20. Edward T. Ramsdell, *The Christian Perspective,* pp. 23 ff. Abingdon Press, 1950.

21. *Ibid.,* p. 31.

22. Flew and MacIntyre, *op. cit.,* p. 41.

23. Will Herberg, "Can Faith and Reason Be Reconciled?" *New Republic,* Vol. 133, No. 17, p. 19. October 24, 1955.

24. E. T. Ramsdell, *op. cit.,* p. 42.

III. The Nature of Revelation

1. For a discussion of the significance of the history of Jesus, **see** Donald M. Baillie, *God Was in Christ*, Ch. II. Charles Scribner's Sons, 1948.

2. John Baillie, *The Idea of Revelation in Recent Thought*, p. 24. Columbia University Press, 1956.

3. See H. Lindsell and C. J. Woodbridge, *A Handbook of Christian Truth*, p. 26. Fleming H. Revell Company, 1953.

4. Victor White, *God the Unknown*, p. 192. Harper & Brothers, 1956.

5. See Edward John Carnell, *An Introduction to Christian Apologetics*, pp. 198–201. Wm. B. Eerdmans Publishing Company, 1948.

6. *Ibid.*, pp. 236–242.

7. Carl F. H. Henry, editor, *Contemporary Evangelical Thought*, p. 272. Channel Press, 1957.

8. John Calvin, *Institutes of the Christian Religion*, tr. by John Allen, Bk. I. Ch. vii. Sec. 4. Presbyterian Board of Christian Education, n.d.

9. *Ibid.*, I. viii.

10. E.g., see I. M. Crombie, "The Possibility of Theological Statements," in Basil Mitchell, *op. cit.*, Ch. II.

11. H. Lindsell and C. Woodbridge, *op. cit.*, pp. 25–26.

12. K. Barth, *Church Dogmatics*, Vol. I, Pt. 2, pp. 529–530.

13. *Ibid.*, p. 513.

14. See J. Baillie, *op. cit.*, Ch. IV; Emil Brunner, *Revelation and Reason*, tr. by Olive Wyon, Chs. 2–13. The Westminster Press, 1946; K. Barth, *Church Dogmatics*, Vol. I, Pt. 2, Ch. iii; Bernhard Anderson, *Rediscovering the Bible*, Chs. 1 and 2. Association Press, 1951.

15. E. Brunner, *Revelation and Reason*, p. 149.

16. *Ibid*.

17. See F. C. Grant, *An Introduction to New Testament Thought*, Ch. 9. Abingdon Press, 1950.

18. Martin Luther, *Commentary on Epistle to the Galatians*, p. 16. Fleming H. Revell Company, n.d.

19. J. Baillie, *op. cit.*, p. 92.

20. E. Brunner, *Revelation and Reason*, p. 168.

IV. How Can We Know that Revelation Is Revelation?

1. John Bennett, "Are There Tests of Revelation?" *Theology Today*, Vol. XII, No. 1, p. 69. April, 1955. I recommend this whole article

as an informative treatment of our problem.

2. E. H. Sugden, *op. cit.*, Vol. I, p. 216.

3. *Ibid.*, pp. 216–217.

4. K. Barth, *Church Dogmatics*, Vol. I, Pt. 2, pp. 1–45.

5. *Ibid.*, p. 3.

6. Edward John Carnell, *Christian Commitment*, pp. 142–143. The Macmillan Company, 1957.

7. E. H. Sugden, *op. cit.*, Vol. I, p. 32.

8. See J. Hick, *op. cit.*, Ch. I.

9. Sören Kierkegaard, *On Authority and Revelation*, tr. by Walter Lowrie. Princeton University Press, 1955.

10. E.g., see E. Brunner, *The Christian Doctrine of Creation and Redemption*, tr. by Olive Wyon, chs. 10–12. The Westminster Press, 1952.

11. Will Herberg, "Biblical Faith and Natural Religion," *Theology Today*, Vol. XI, No. 4, pp. 460–467. January, 1955.

12. J. Hick, *op. cit.*, Ch. 6.

V. God's Immanence and Transcendence

1. See J. G. Machen, *Christianity and Liberalism*, pp. 99–100. Wm. B. Eerdmans Publishing Company, 1946.

2. E. J. Carnell, *An Introduction to Christian Apologetics*, p. 268.

3. J. G. Machen, *op. cit.*, p. 109.

4. E. J. Carnell, *An Introduction to Christian Apologetics*, pp. 236–242.

5. E. J. Carnell, *The Theology of Reinhold Niebuhr*, p. 19. Wm. B. Eerdmans Publishing Company, 1950.

6. W. N. Clarke, *An Outline of Christian Theology*, p. 131. Charles Scribner's Sons, 1914.

7. *Ibid.*, p. 130.

8. *Ibid.*, p. 38.

9. C. F. H. Henry, *op. cit.*, p. 272.

10. J. Macmurray, *The Self as Agent*, p. 118. Harper & Brothers, 1957.

11. E. Brunner, *The Christian Doctrine of Creation and Redemption*, pp. 153–154.

12. Augustine, *On the Gospel of St. John*, II:10.

13. Augustine, *Of Genesis*, V:23.

14. Augustine, *On the Trinity*, III:5–6.

15. J. Maritain, *Approaches to God*, tr. by P. O'Reilly, p. 38. Harper & Brothers, 1954.

16. J. Calvin, *op cit.*, I. xvi. 7.

17. *Ibid.*, III. xxiii. 8. See also III. xxiii. 12–14.

18. Harry Emerson Fosdick, editor, *Rufus Jones Speaks to Our Time*, p. 7. The Macmillan Company, 1951.

19. See *The Christian Century*, Vol. LXXIV, No. 51, pp. 1512–1513. December 18, 1957.

VI. Sin

1. J. G. Machen, *op. cit.*, pp. 105–106.

2. Lyman Abbott, *The Evolution of Christianity*, p. 255. Doubleday & Co., Inc., 1892.

3. W. N. Clarke, *op. cit.*, p. 227.

4. *Ibid.*, p. 244.

5. *Ibid.*, p. 245.

6. H. Lindsell and C. Woodbridge, *op. cit.*, p. 89.

7. E.g., see Reinhold Niebuhr, *The Nature and Destiny of Man*, Vol. I. Charles Scribner's Sons, 1941. Emil Brunner, *Man in Revolt*, tr. by Olive Wyon. The Westminster Press, 1947. D. R. Davies, *On to Orthodoxy*. The Macmillan Company, 1949.

8. J. Calvin, *op. cit.*, III. xxiii. 3.

9. Quoted by Paul Ramsey, in Kegley and Bretall (editors): *Reinhold Niebuhr: His Religious, Social, and Political Thought*, pp. 118–119. The Macmillan Company, 1956.

10. Reinhold Niebuhr, *The Irony of American History*, p. 17. Charles Scribner's Sons, 1952.

11. See particularly R. Niebuhr, *The Nature and Destiny of Man*, Vol. I, Ch. 7.

12. D. Riesman, N. Glazer, and R. Denney, *The Lonely Crowd* (abridged), pp. 28 ff. Doubleday & Co., Inc., 1954.

13. *Ibid.*, pp. 34 ff.

14. C. S. Lewis, *Christian Behaviour*, pp. 45–46. The Macmillan Company, 1943.

VII. Salvation

1. Paul Holmer, "Modern Theology — Another Evasion?" *The Christian Century*, Vol. LXXV, No. 4, pp. 101–103. January 22, 1958.

2. K. Barth, *Church Dogmatics*, Vol. I, Pt. 2, p. 792.

3. *Ibid.*, pp. 401–402.

4. *Ibid.*, p. 793.

5. E. H. Sugden, *op. cit.*, Vol. I, pp. 48–49.

6. For a complete description of these theories, see Gustaf Aulén, *Christus Victor,* tr. by A. G. Hebert. The Macmillan Company, 1951.

7. E.g., see Matt. 12:28–29; 20:28; John 12:31; I Cor. 6:20; II Cor. 13:4; Gal. 1:4; 4:3–7; Col. 2:13–15; I Tim. 2:6; Heb. 2:14–16; I Peter 1:18–21; I John 3:8.

8. E.g., see Rom. 3:25; II Cor. 5:21; I Peter 2:24.

9. E.g., see Luke 15:11–32; John 3:16–21; II Cor. 5:18–20; Col. 1:19–29; I John 4:13–21.

10. Will Herberg, *Protestant, Catholic, Jew,* p. 98. Doubleday & Co., Inc., 1955.

11. William Hordern, *Christianity, Communism, and History.* Abingdon Press, 1954.

VIII. Conclusion

1. K. Barth, *Church Dogmatics,* Vol. I, Pt. 1, p. 35.

2. *Ibid.*, p. 246.

3. *Ibid.*, p. 185.

4. Harry Emerson Fosdick, *The Living of These Days,* p. 247. Harper & Brothers, 1956.

SUGGESTED READINGS
WORKS OF AN INTRODUCTORY NATURE

Aulén, Gustaf, *Christus Victor.* The Macmillan Company, 1951.

———, *The Faith of the Christian Church.* Muhlenberg Press, 1948.

Baillie, Donald M., *God Was in Christ.* Charles Scribner's Sons, 1948.

Baillie, John, *The Idea of Revelation in Recent Thought.* Columbia University Press, 1956.

Barth, Karl, *The Knowledge of God.* Charles Scribner's Sons, 1939.

———, *Christ and Adam.* Harper & Brothers, 1957.

Brunner, Emil, *The Divine-Human Encounter.* The Westminster Press, 1943.

———, *The Scandal of Christianity.* The Westminster Press, 1951.

Heinecken, Martin, *The Moment Before God.* Muhlenberg Press, 1956.

Hick, John, *Faith and Knowledge.* Cornell University Press, 1957.

Horton, Walter M., *Christian Theology: An Ecumenical Approach.* Harper & Brothers, 1955.

Hubben, William, *Four Prophets of Our Destiny.* The Macmillan Company, 1952.

Hutchison, John, *Faith, Reason, and Existence.* Oxford University Press, 1956.

Johnson, Robert, *The Meaning of Christ.* The Westminster Press, 1958.

Kierkegaard, Sören, *Training in Christianity.* Princeton University Press, 1944.

Lewis, Edwin, *The Biblical Faith and Christian Freedom.* The Westminster Press, 1953.

Miller, Alexander, *The Renewal of Man.* Doubleday & Co., Inc., 1955.

Nash, Arnold (editor), *Protestant Thought in the Twentieth Century.* The Macmillan Company, 1951.

Niebuhr, Reinhold, *Beyond Tragedy.* Charles Scribner's Sons, 1938.

———, *Faith and History.* Charles Scribner's Sons, 1949.

———, *The Self and the Dramas of History.* Charles Scribner's Sons, 1955.

Niebuhr, H. Richard, *The Meaning of Revelation.* The Macmillan Company, 1941.

Ramsdell, Edward T., *The Christian Perspective.* Abingdon Press, 1950.

Read, David H. C., *The Christian Faith.* Charles Scribner's Sons, 1956.

Wolf, William J., *Man's Knowledge of God.* Doubleday & Co., Inc., 1955.

Zuurdeeg, Willem F., *An Analytical Philosophy of Religion.* Abingdon Press, 1958.

FOR MORE ADVANCED READING

Barth, Karl, *Church Dogmatics.* (This whole work is in the process of being published in English by Charles Scribner's Sons.)

Brunner, Emil, *Revelation and Reason.* The Westminster Press, 1946.

———, *The Christian Doctrine of God.* The Westminster Press, 1950.

———, *The Christian Doctrine of Creation and Redemption.* The Westminster Press, 1952.

Kierkegaard, Sören, *Philosophical Fragments.* Princeton University Press, 1936.

———, *Concluding Unscientific Postscript.* Princeton University Press, 1941.

Niebuhr, Reinhold, *The Nature and Destiny of Man.* Charles Scribner's Sons, Vol. I (1941) and Vol. II (1943).

Index

Abbott, L., 125
Abelard, P., 150
Allport, G., 153
Analytic philosophy, 10, 26–30, 37–38, 62–63, 89, 98, 99
Anderson, B., 169
Anselm, 145–146
Anxiety, 133–137, 155
Apologetics, 23, 86, 92, 97–99
A posteriori, 78–83, 87, 130
A priori, 78–83, 87, 88, 119, 130
Aquinas, T., 26, 39, 97, 117
Aristotle, 79
Atheism, 41–42, 88–89, 139
Atonement, 14, 23, 142–151
Augustine, 18, 41, 88, 116, 156
Aulén, G., 23, 35, 143, 172
Ayer, A. J., 27, 28

Baillie, D. M., 23, 169
Baillie, J., 23, 55, 68, 72, 169
Baptism, 152–153
Barth, K., 20, 21–22, 24, 25, 26, 29, 31, 33, 35–36, 37, 38, 62, 63, 65, 67–68, 73, 76, 77, 78–81, 87–88, 89, 105, 126, 141–142, 152, 160, 162, 163–164, 169
Beardsley, M. C., 168
Bennett, J. C., 24, 76
Bible: inerrancy of, 14, 18, 53, 56, 57–61, 64, 66, 67, 73, 86, 87, 107–108, 110; as revelation, 65–75, 82, 92
Biblical criticism, 12, 15, 53–54, 59, 66, 67, 74, 86, 107–108, 113
Brunner, E., 20, 22, 31, 62, 68, 69–70, 73, 105, 112, 152, 153, 169, 170, 171

Buber, M., 11, 22, 62
Bultmann, R., 24–25, 54

Calvin, J., 48, 60–61, 73, 117–118, 131–132, 152, 156, 162
Carnap, R., 27
Carnell, E. J., 81, 105, 106, 107, 169
Casserley, J. V. L., 28
Chesterton, G. K., 42
Christ, Jesus: as incarnation, 54, 61, 83, 85, 87, 97, 101, 106, 115, 143, 146, 153; as Lord, 97, 145; as Messiah, 69, 86; as revelation, 19, 47–48, 61, 64, 65, 68, 69, 70, 71, 73, 74, 87, 94, 97, 118, 119, 120, 131, 132, 150; as Second Adam, 129–131; divinity of, 65, 70–71, 83, 86, 108; humanity of, 65–66; resurrection of, 143, 145; teachings of, 70, 71; work of, 71, 72, 81, 101–102, 142–151, 157–158, 159
Clarke, W. N., 109–110, 125–126
Confirmation, 153
Conservative theology, 15–19, 23, 25, 56, 57, 58, 60, 66, 67, 73, 86, 87, 106–107, 112, 115, 125–126, 129, 131, 142, 161–162
Creation, 12, 60, 75, 104, 105–106, 110, 114, 116, 117, 119
Credentia, 34–35, 39, 56, 72
Creeds, 15, 63, 67, 69, 94, 165
Crombie, I. M., 169

Davies, D. R., 23, 171
De Sua, F., 40
DeWolf, L. H., 34, 167

Ecumenical movement, 12, 145, 165
Eschatology, 105, 121–123
Evolution, 12, 14, 60, 107, 108, 112, 116, 124
Existentialism, 24, 26, 27, 29, 88, 144–145

Faith, definition of, 33–35
Fall of man, 12, 125, 128–131
Ferré, N., 24
Feuerbach, L., 89
Fides, 34–35, 44, 49, 51, 94–102, 104
Fiducia, 34–35, 51, 94–95
Forsyth, P. T., 21, 23
Fosdick, H. E., 164, 171
Fox, G., 74
Frame of reference, 40, 42–46, 48, 50–52, 64, 76, 94, 97
Freud, S., 89
Fundamentalism, 13–19, 53–54, 56, 57, 59, 60, 66, 106–107, 108, 109, 110, 113–114, 161–162

God: freedom of, 77, 111, 118, 119–120; image of, 20, 107, 112, 129, 136; knowledge of, 19–20, 22, 36–38, 39, 53–75, 79–94, 118; personal nature of, 55, 62–63, 68, 82, 111; providence of, 106, 118; proofs of, 26, 27, 38, 45–47, 116–117; Word of, 21–22, 33, 35, 60, 61, 62, 65, 66–67, 74, 77, 90, 93, 108, 162, 163
Grace, 67–68, 77, 85, 158, 164
Graham, Billy, 16
Grant, F. C., 169
Gregory the Great, 143
Guilt, 146–149, 150

Hare, R. M., 168
Heidegger, M., 24
Heinecken, M., 32–33
Henry, C., 60, 112
Herberg, W., 47, 89, 153
Hick, J., 27, 29, 96, 104, 170
Holmer, P., 141
Holy Spirit, 22, 54, 60, 61, 74, 85, 93
Horton, W. M., 24, 162
Hospers, J., 168
Hume, D., 27, 37, 43, 96, 98
Hutchison, J., 41

Idealist philosophy, 15, 24–29, 96, 111, 162
Idolatry, 63, 74, 87–90, 105, 138, 139, 165
I-Thou relation, 22, 62–63, 99, 121

Jones, R., 120–121

Kant, I., 27, 98
Kierkegaard, S., 20–21, 26, 29, 32–33, 59, 62, 70, 83, 85–86, 133
Kingdom of God, 111, 121, 122, 130
Kraft, V., 40

Lewis, C. S., 128, 139–140
Liberal theology, 14–19, 22, 24, 25, 26, 31, 39, 53–54, 55, 66, 70, 86, 108–111, 112, 113, 115, 120, 121, 125–126, 141, 142, 158, 161–162, 163, 164
Lindsell, H., 169, 171
Logical positivism, 27, 28, 89
Luther, M., 23, 28, 34, 35, 36, 48, 61, 70, 73, 89, 90–91, 93, 120, 143, 145, 149, 152, 156, 162, 165

Machen, J. G., 106–107, 125, 170
MacKay, J., 24

Macmurray, J., 112
Maritain, J., 11, 117
Metaphysics, 27–30, 38, 75, 88, 89, 101
Miracles, 12, 54, 73, 83, 106–108, 113–115, 116, 117, 125
Mises, R. Von, 41
Mitchell, B., 30, 169

Natural theology, 22, 31, 33, 36–38, 75
Naturalism, 25, 103–104
Neo-orthodoxy, 15–17, 24, 31, 162
New Reformation theology, definition of, 17–20
Niebuhr, H. R., 24, 62
Niebuhr, Reinhold, 11, 20, 21, 23–24, 25, 50, 91, 113, 128, 133, 135, 139, 141, 163, 171
Nygren, A., 22–23

Occam, William of, 28
Oman, J., 21, 23
Original sin, 125–126, 129–132, 136–137, 163
Orthodoxy, 12, 126, 163, 165
Otto, R., 33

Paradox, 21, 32–33, 83
Pascal, B., 47, 155
Pauck, W., 24
Paul, 12, 34, 71, 72, 77, 98, 106, 140, 143, 145, 149, 155
Perspective, 42–45, 49, 50–52, 64, 74, 76, 91, 92, 93–94, 98, 118, 127–128, 159
Peter, 48, 64–65, 68–69, 73
Phenix, P., 121–122
Predestination, 117–118, 131–132, 152
Progress, 13, 50, 121, 122, 124, 128

Racial discrimination, 126, 138, 141, 158–159
Ramsdell, E. T., 10, 43, 44, 52
Rauschenbusch, W., 21
Reason, definition of, 32
Riesman, D., 138–139
Ritschl, A., 53
Roman Catholicism, 34, 56–57, 59, 66, 67, 69–70, 73, 165

Salvation by grace, 19, 90–91, 151–156
Salvation through faith, 72, 151–156
Sanctification, 155–157, 159
Sartre, J. P., 128, 144–145
Schleiermacher, F., 53
Science and religion, 12, 14, 15, 60, 92, 107, 108–109, 113–115, 116, 118
Smart, J. C., 46–47, 100
Supernaturalism, 104, 110, 115, 116

Temple, W., 21, 23, 62
Theology, 11–12, 63, 72–73, 94, 160–161, 163–166
Tillich, P., 11, 24–25, 26, 38, 47, 54

Van Til, C., 105

Wesley, J., 35, 77, 82, 142, 149, 155, 162
White, M., 27
White, V., 56–57, 68
Whitehead, A. N., 26, 111
Wisdom, J., 62–63
Woodbridge, C. J., 169, 171

Zuurdeeg, W. F., 10, 30